Colormazen

Large Mandala Pattern Coloring Book

Volume 1

Designed by

CAROL BELL

Colormazen

Copyright © 2018 Carol Bell

All rights reserved. This book or any portion thereof may not be reproduced or used in any manner whatsoever without the express written permission of the publisher.

http://www.colormazen.com/

ISBN-13: 978-1987476682

ISBN: 1987476689

DEDICATION

To my Grandchildren

Shannon, Liam, Grace, Stanley, Ollie, George, Émilie, Jake and Joseph.

Coloring Instructions and Tips

This book may be colored using colored pencils, felt tipped pens, gel pens, markers, pastels and paints.

All designs in this book have been printed on the odd numbered pages.

The even pages have been left deliberately blank as some coloring mediums such as felt tip pens will bleed through onto the reverse side of the paper.

Always test markers or gel pens to check to see if it bleeds through or leaves a mark.

To make extra sure you do not get bleed through place a blank piece of thick paper or card behind the design that you are coloring and the next page.

If you are an experienced colorist you could use shading or the blending of two colors to complete these simple designs.

Or use the white space to expand the mandala or draw your own patterns.

Have fun and color outside the lines.

Happy Coloring!

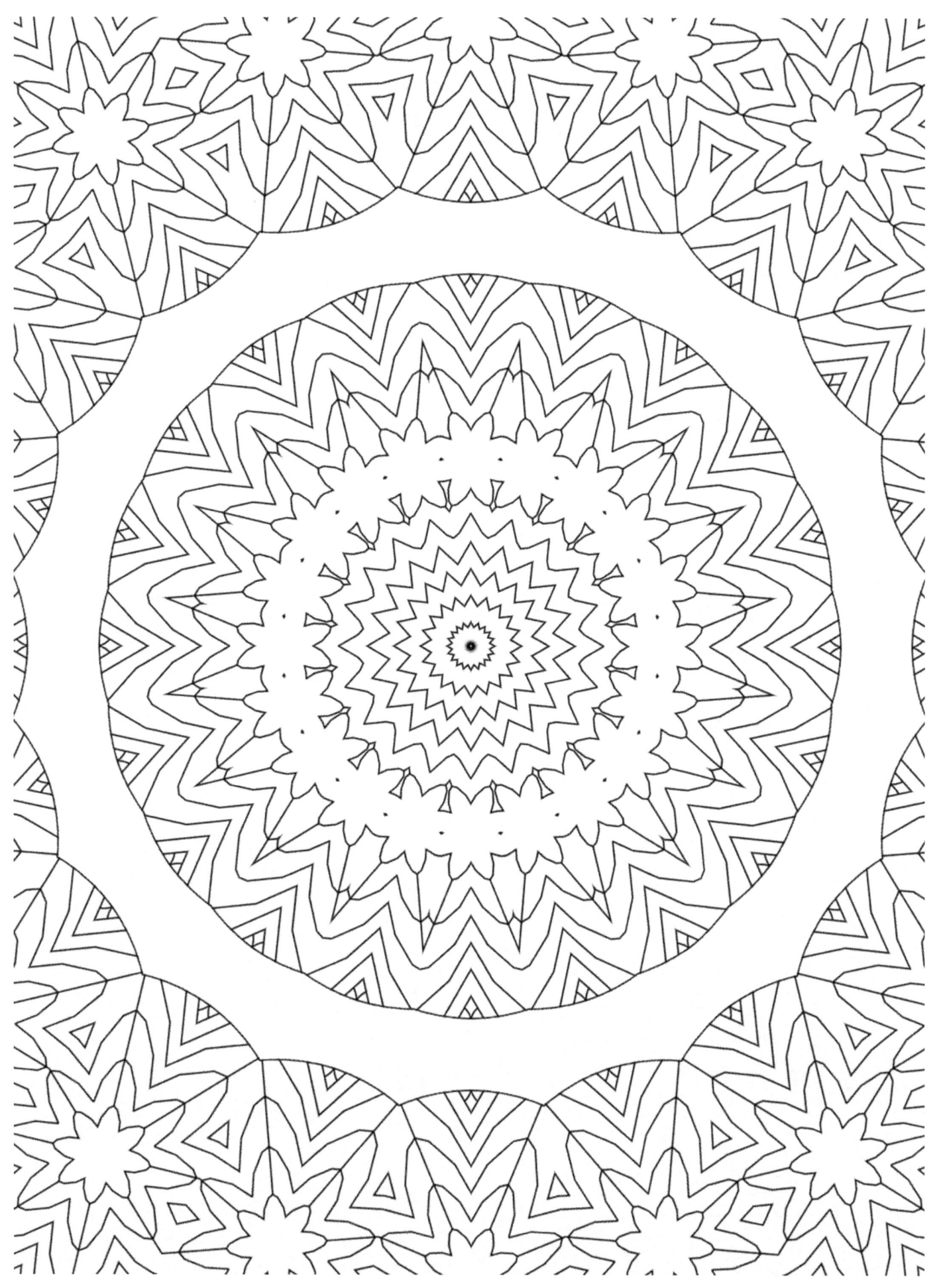

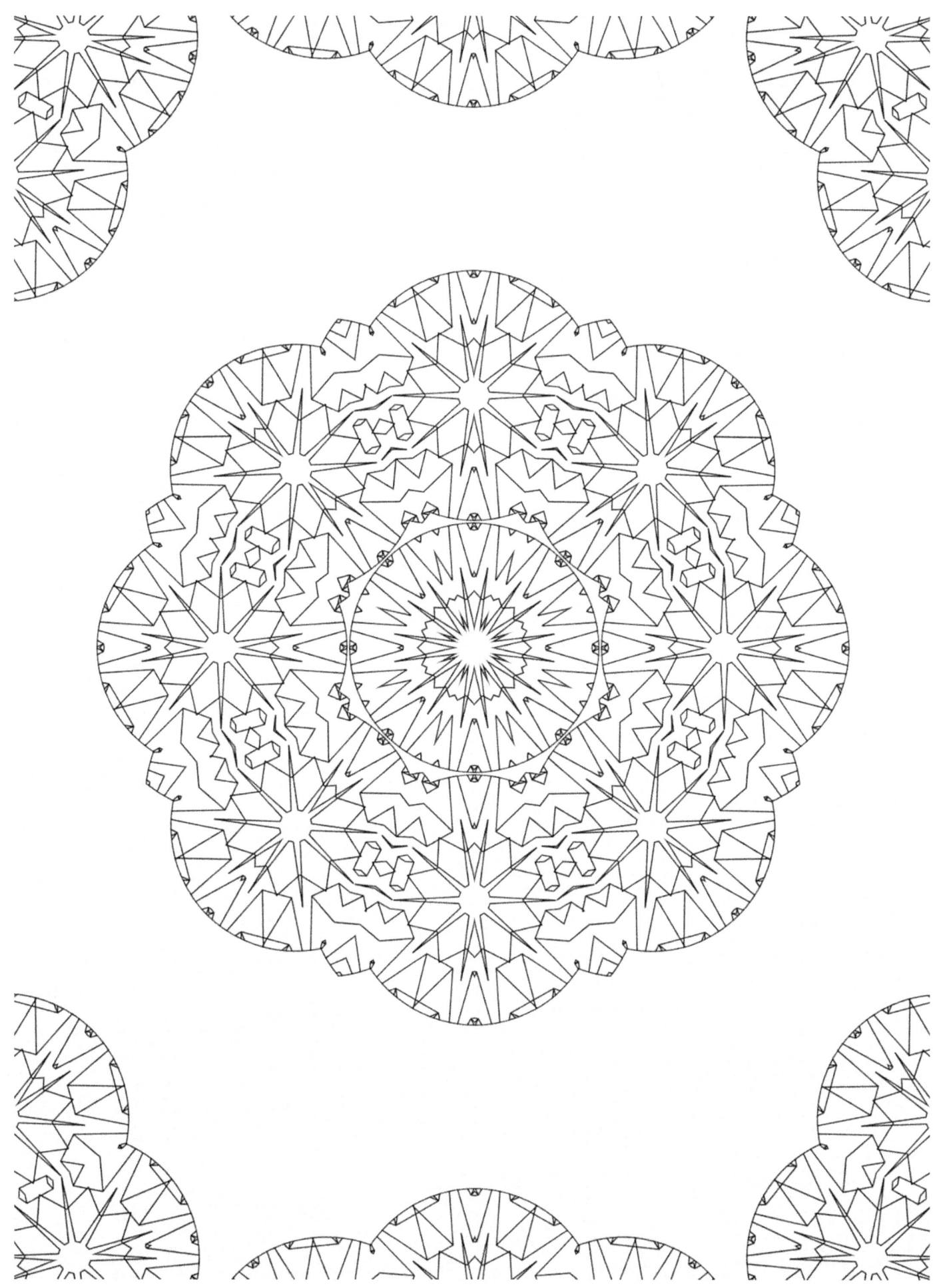

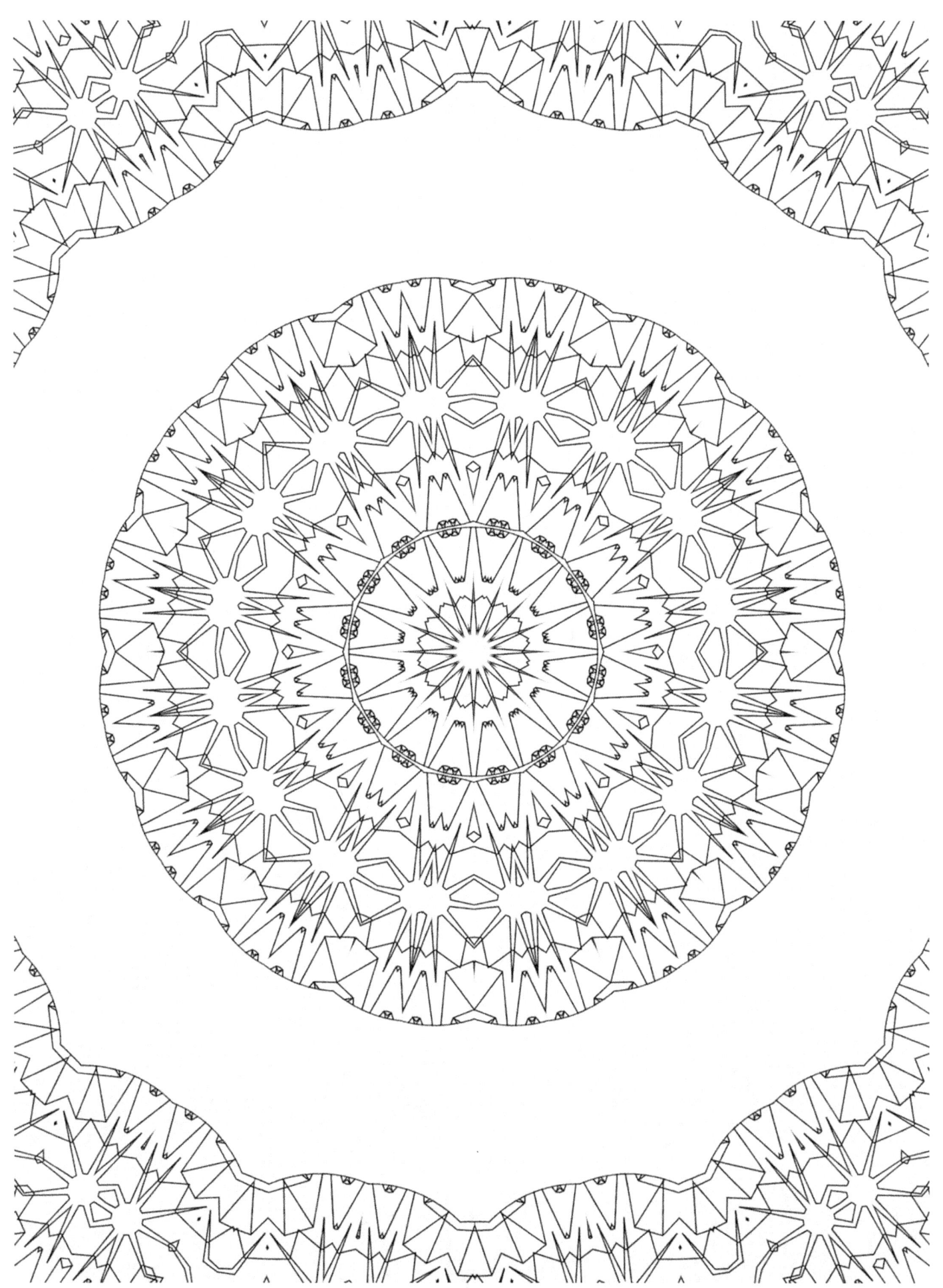

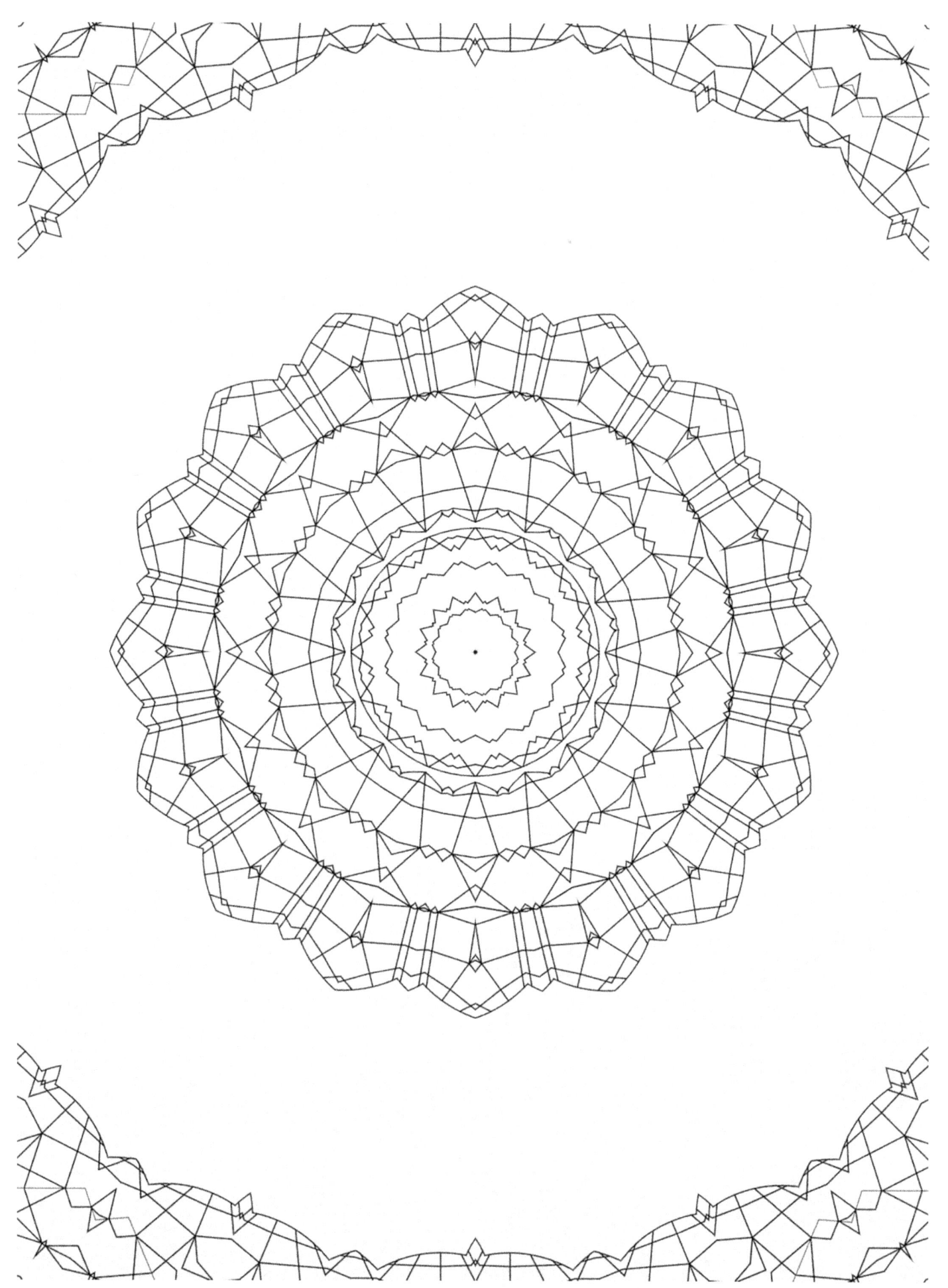

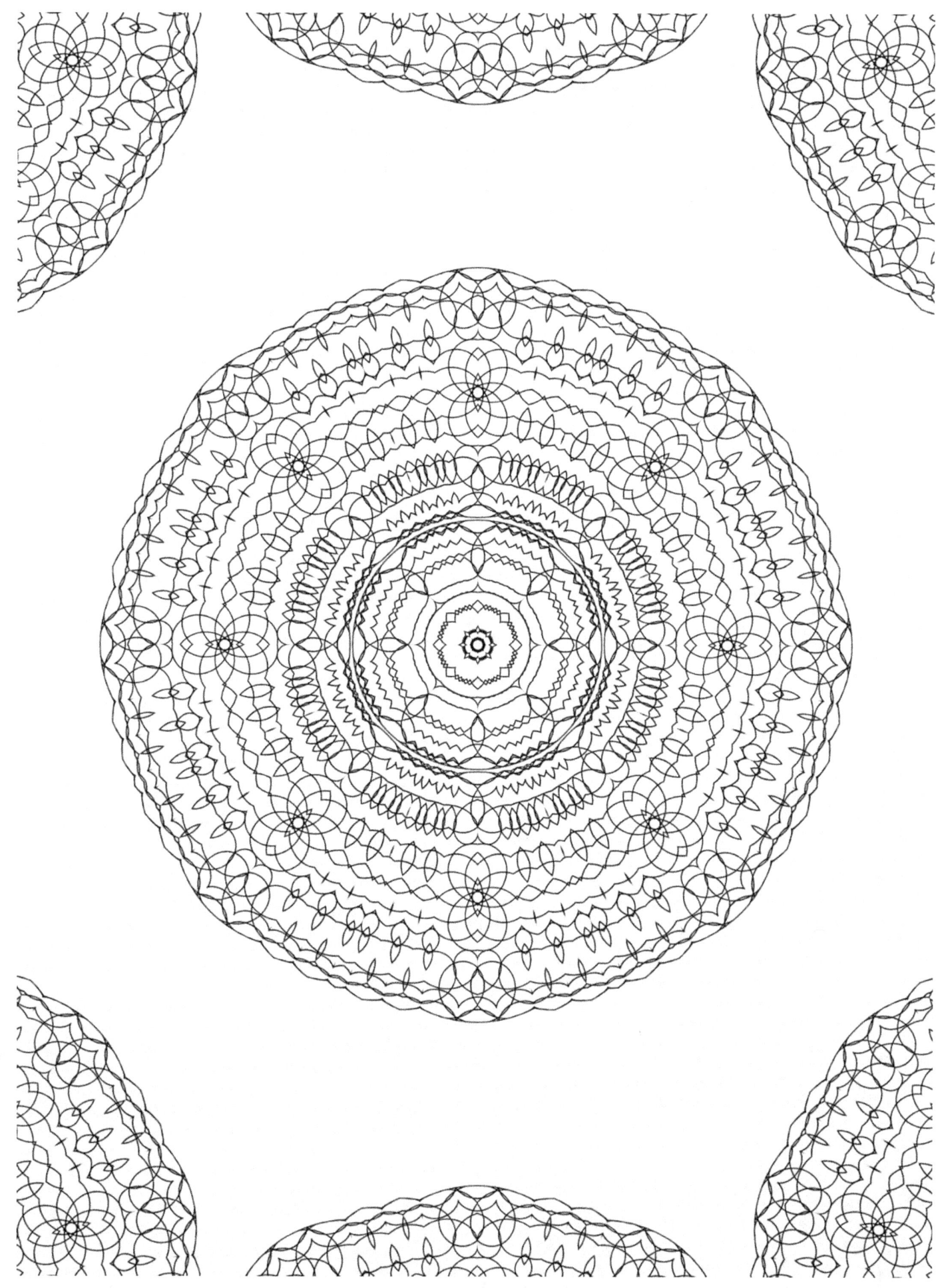

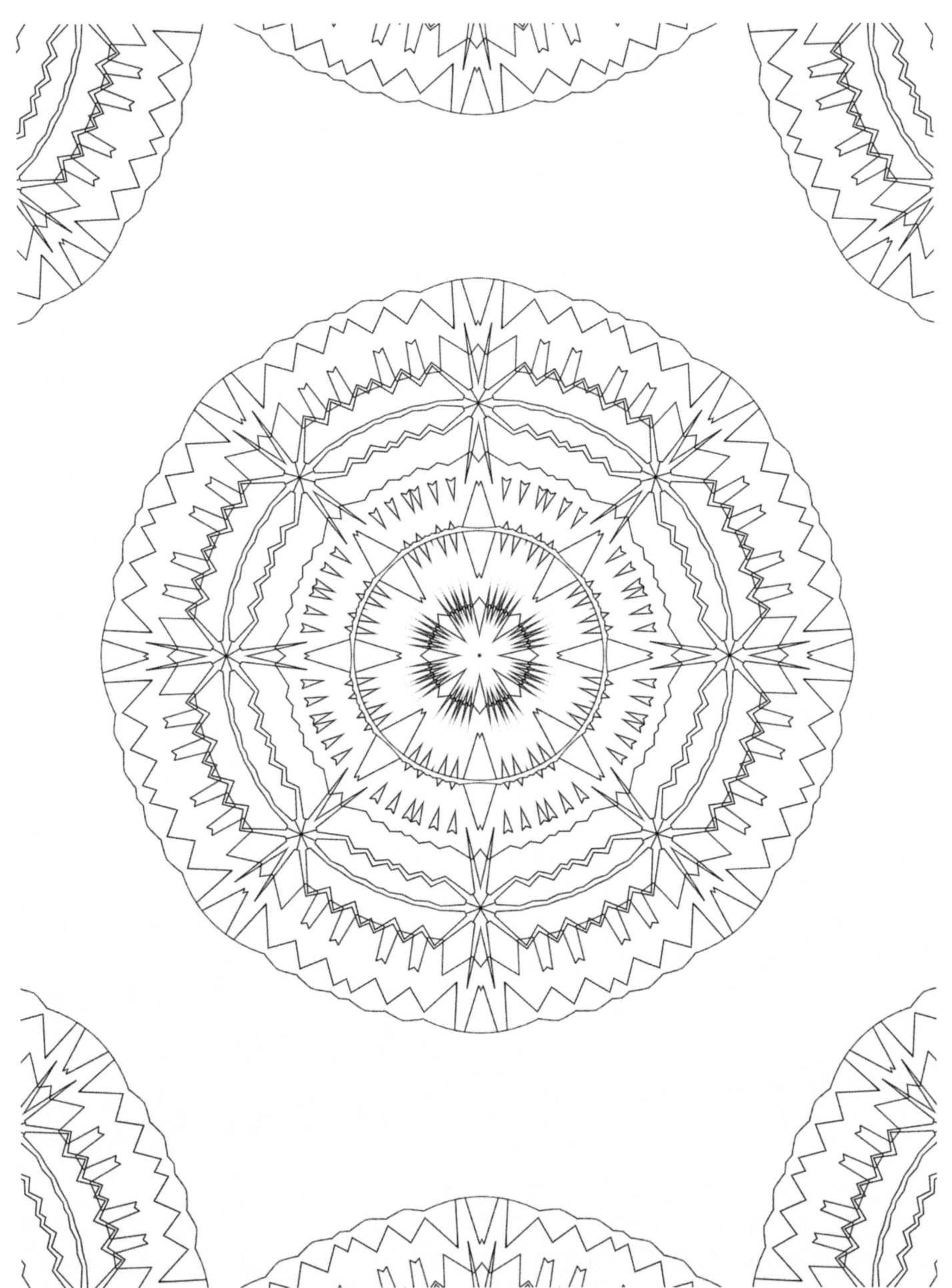

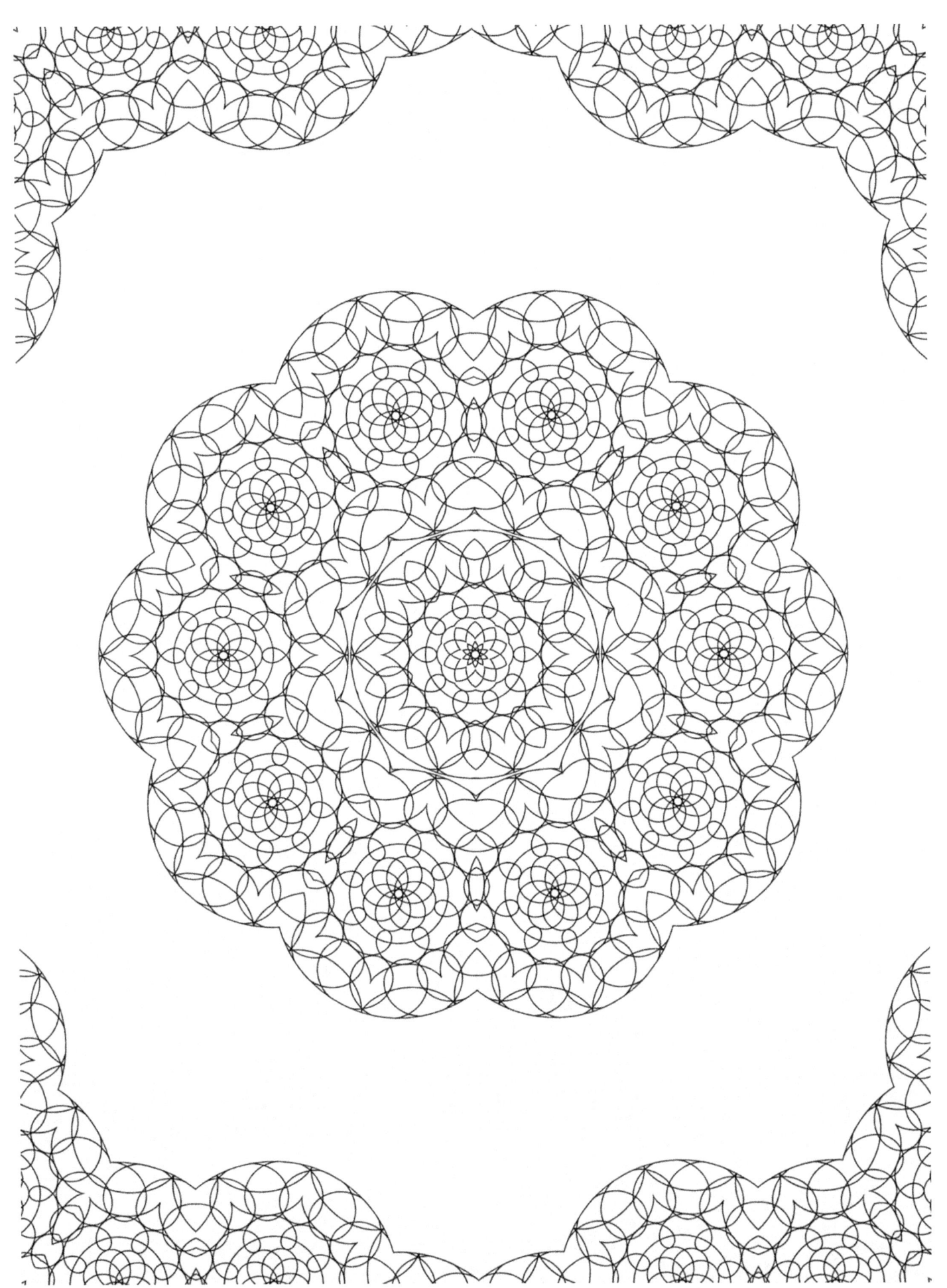

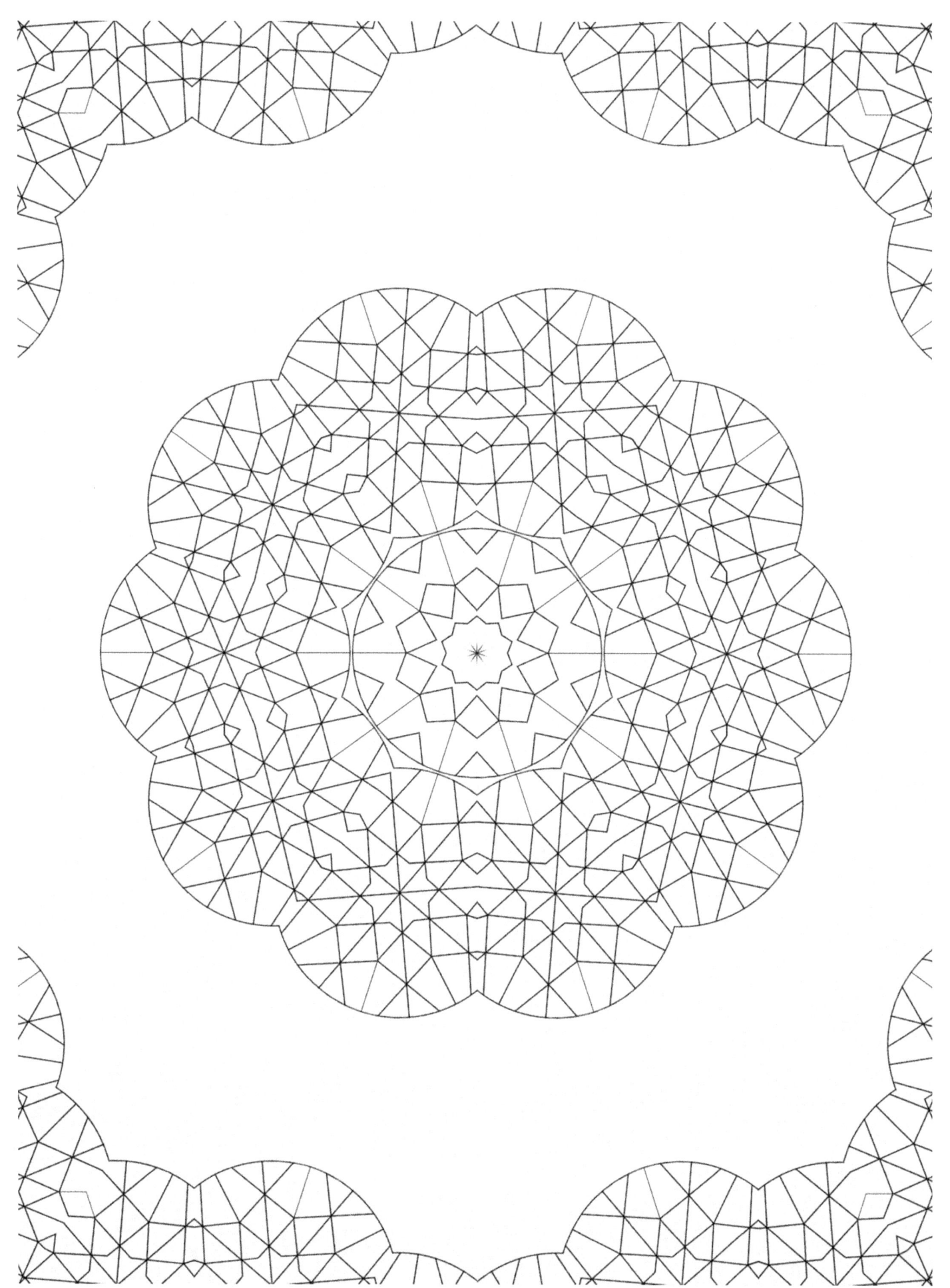

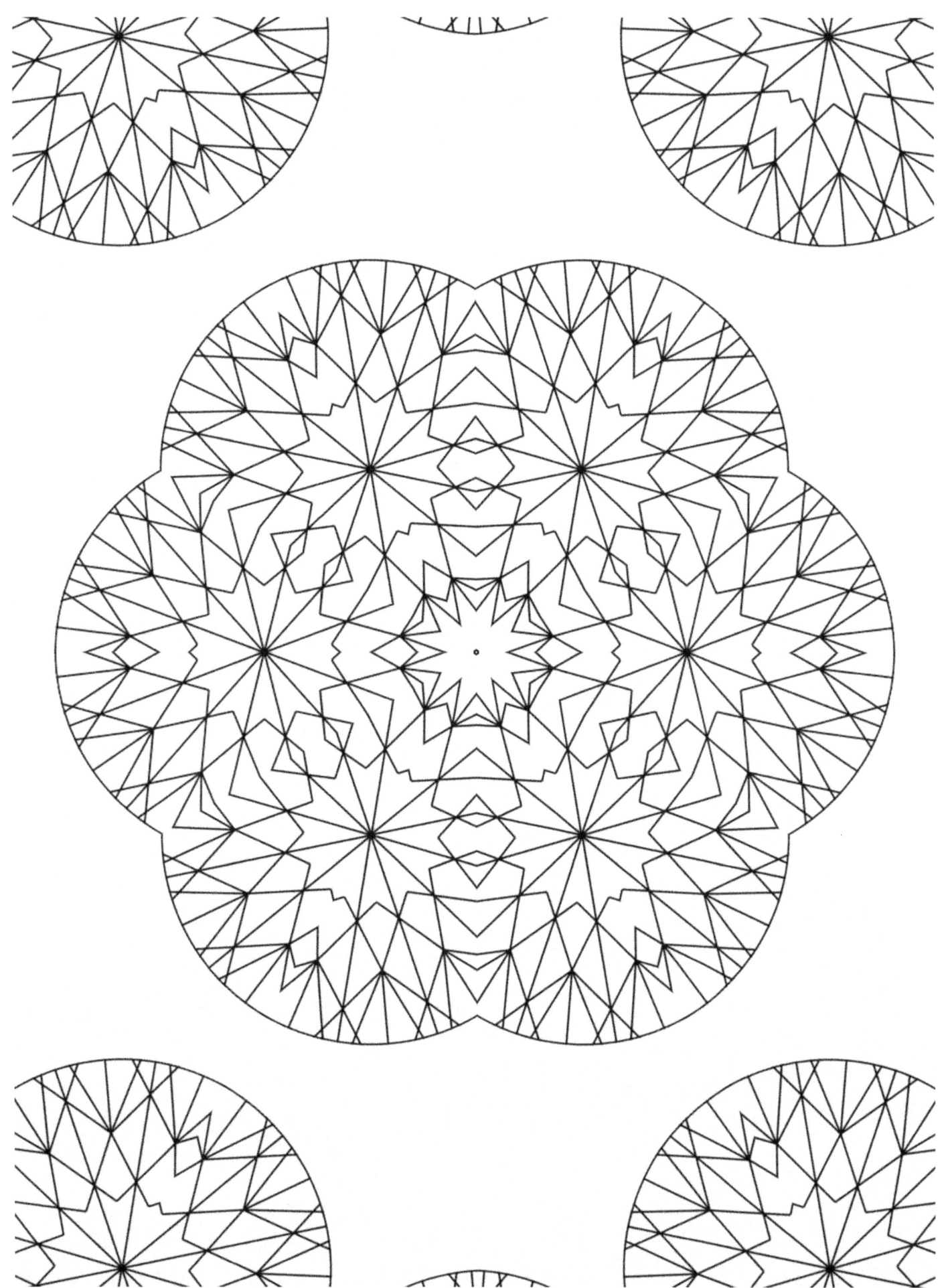

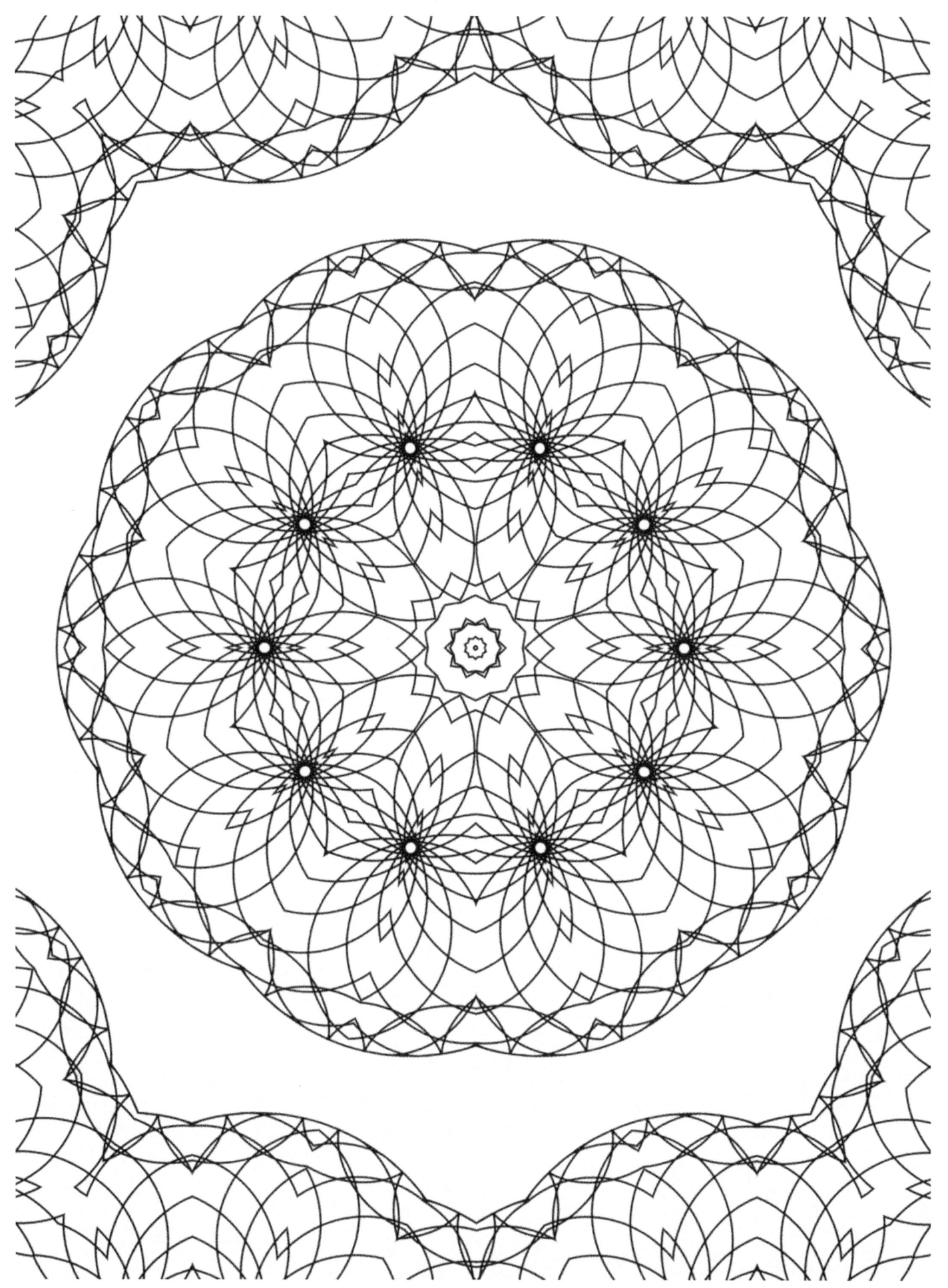

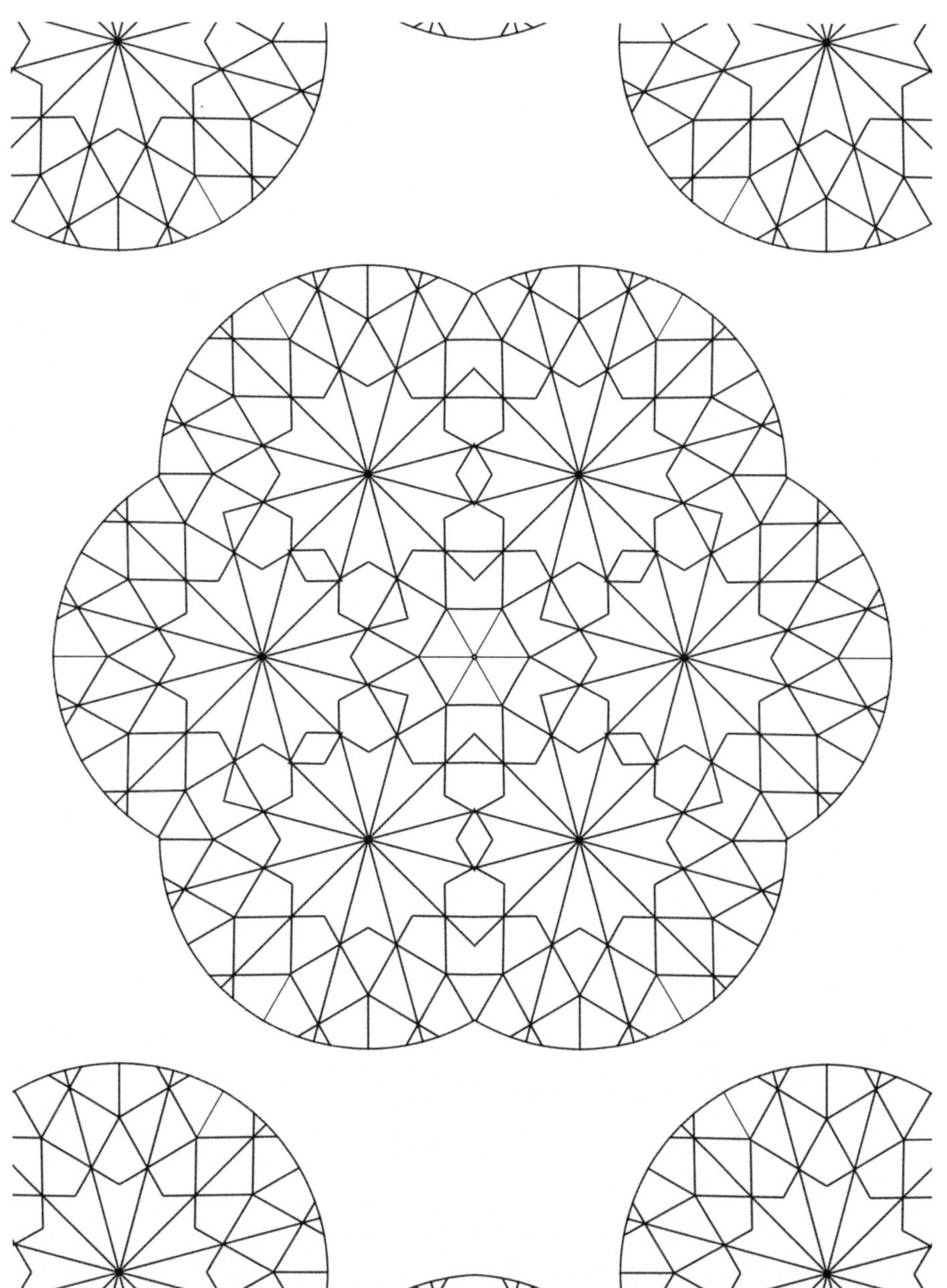

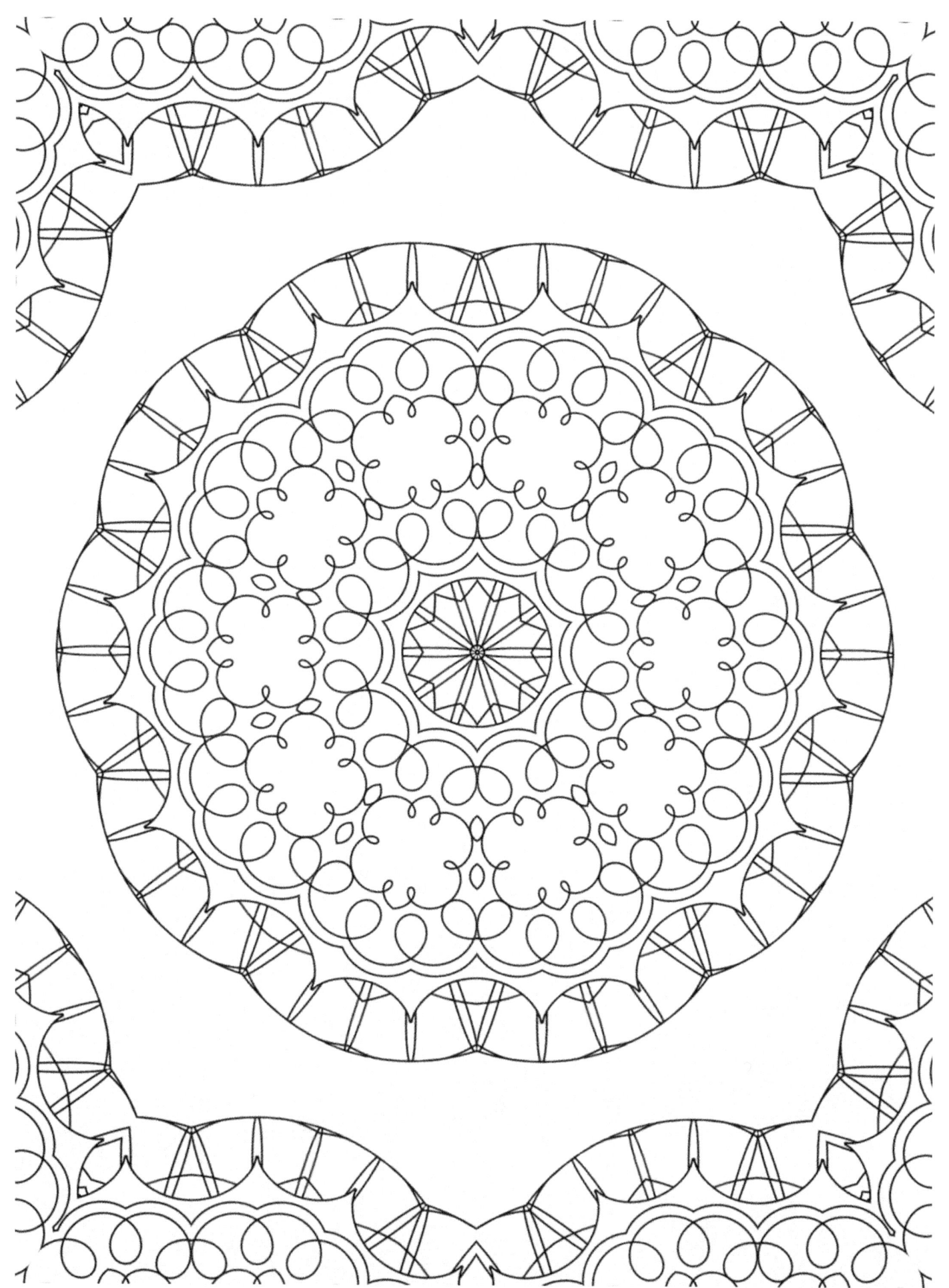

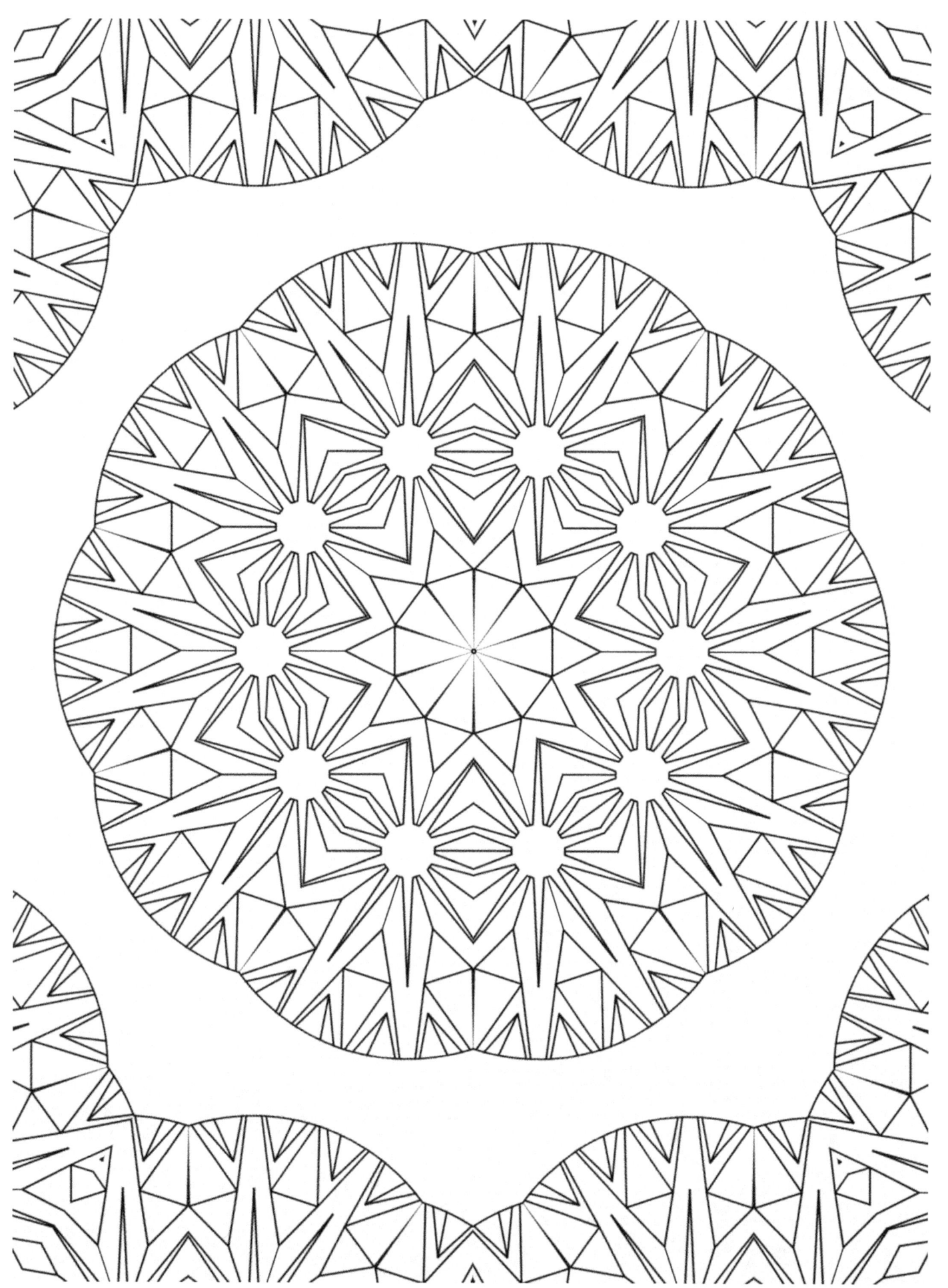

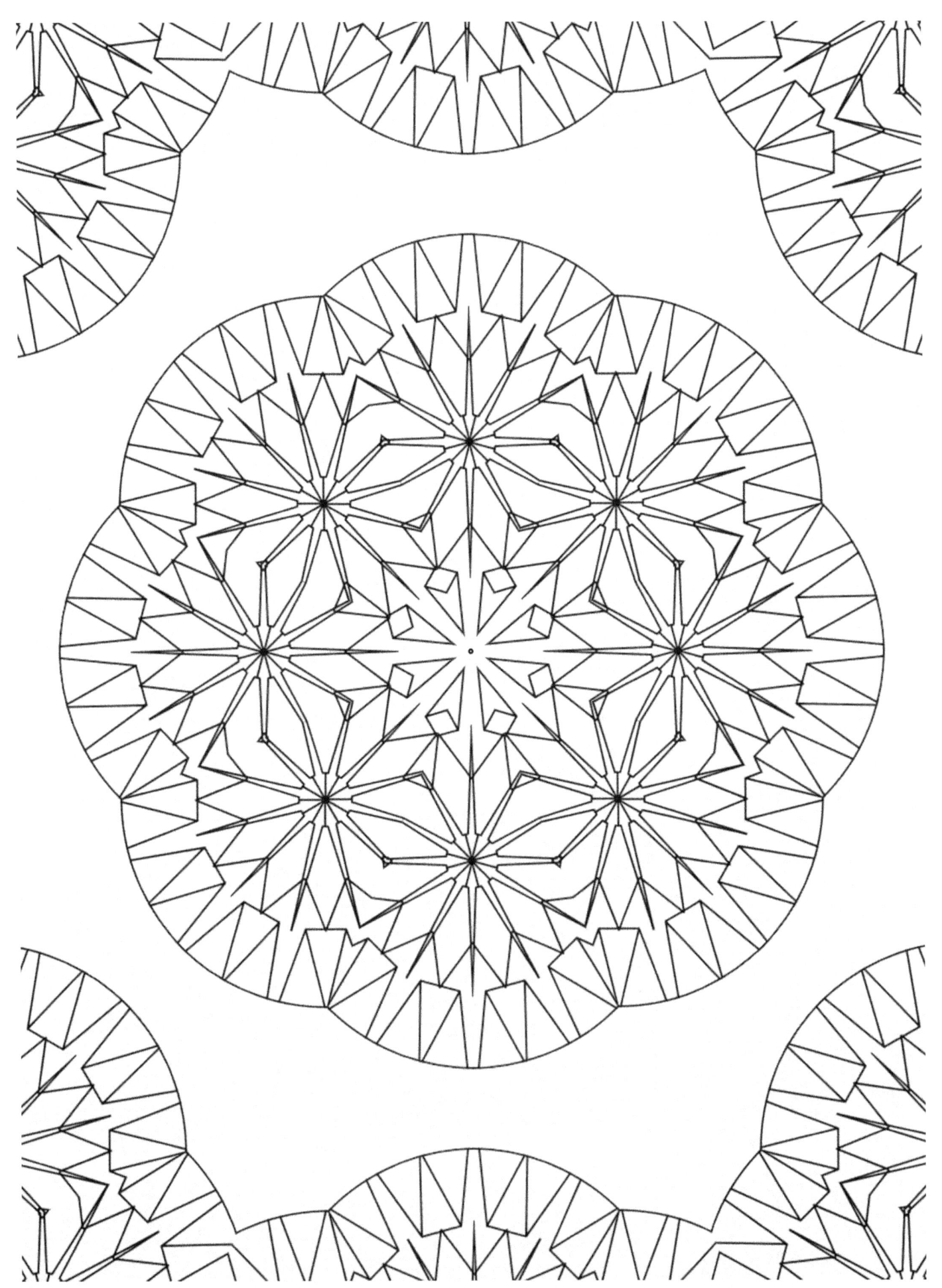

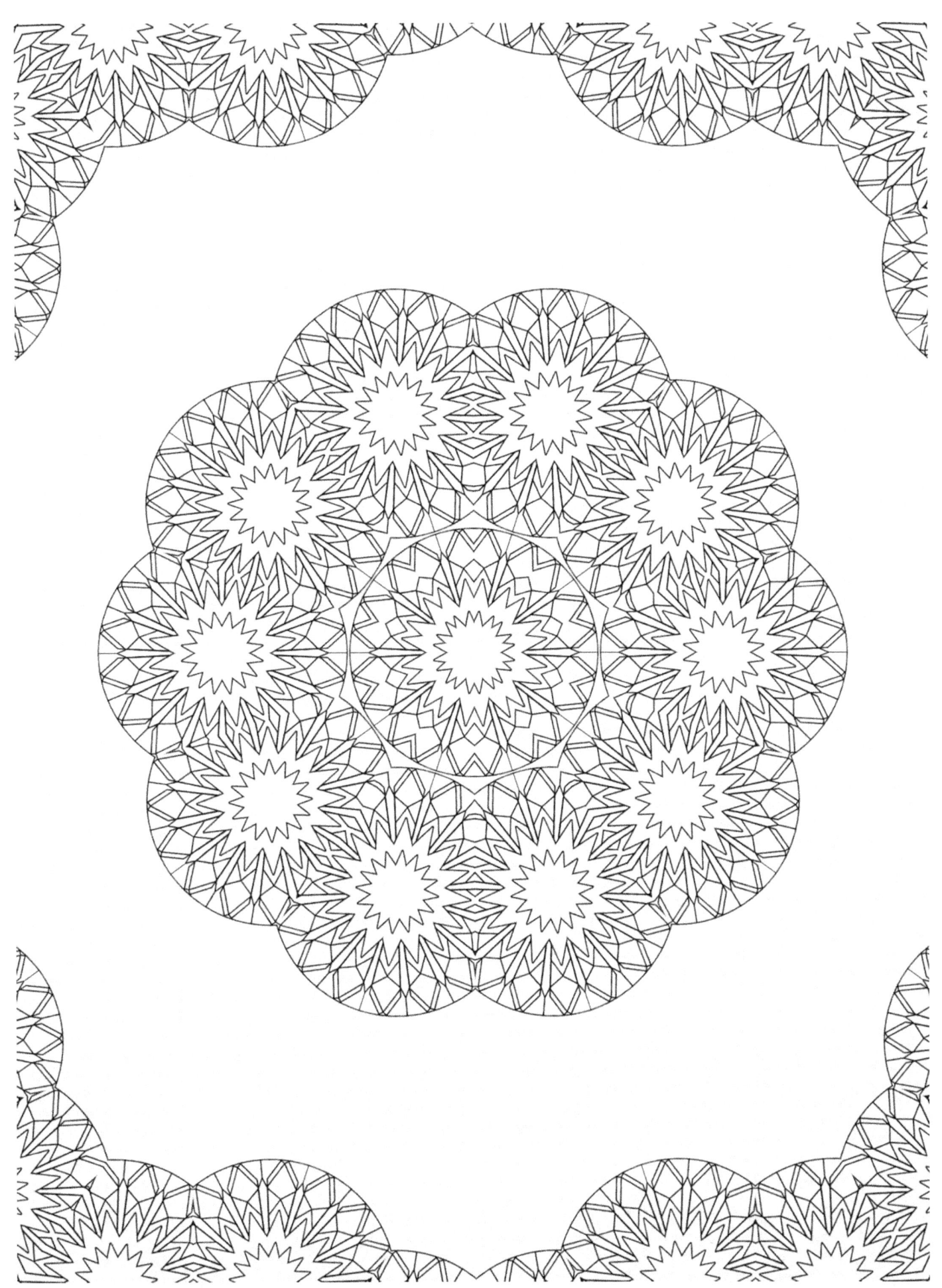

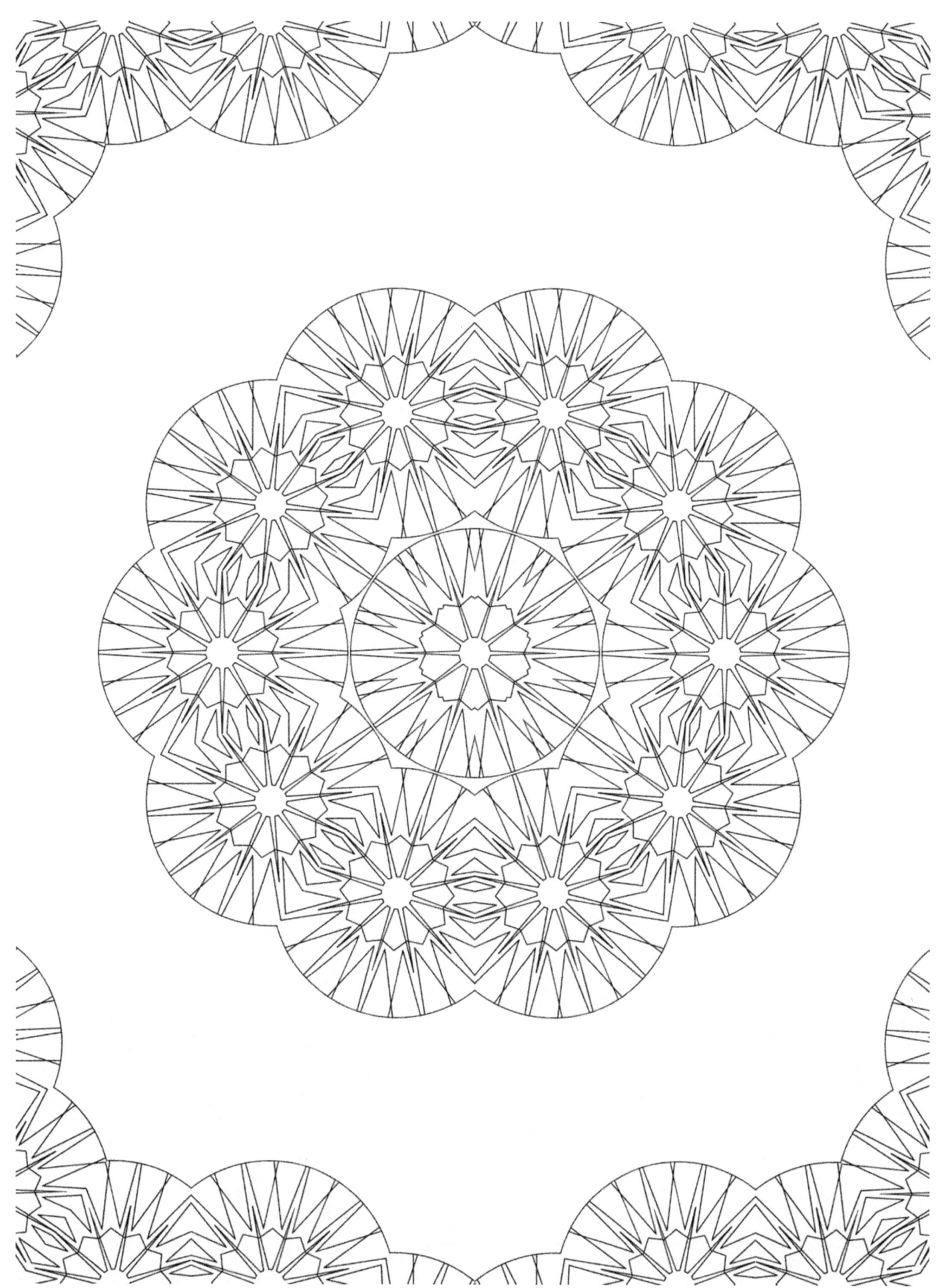

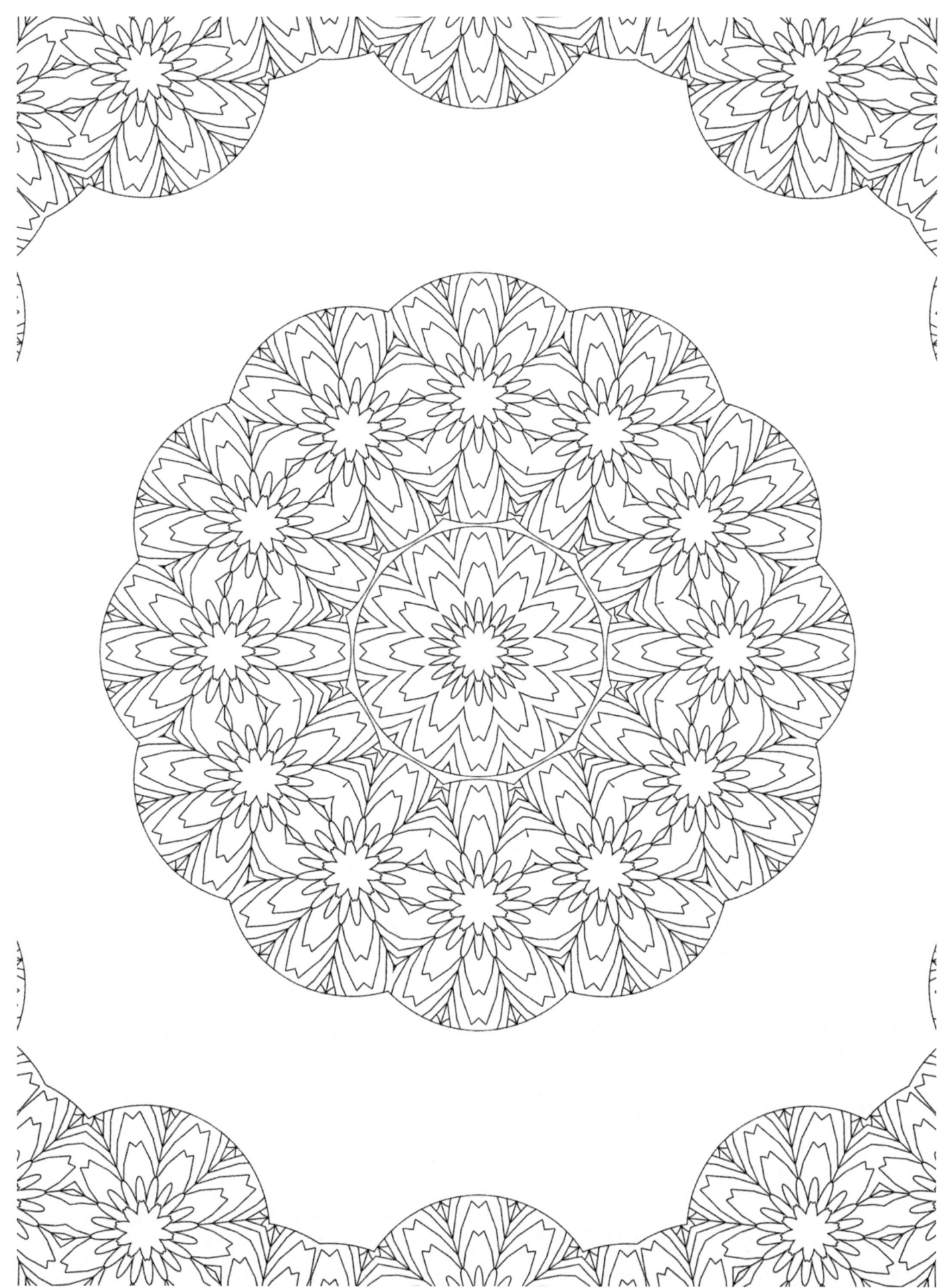

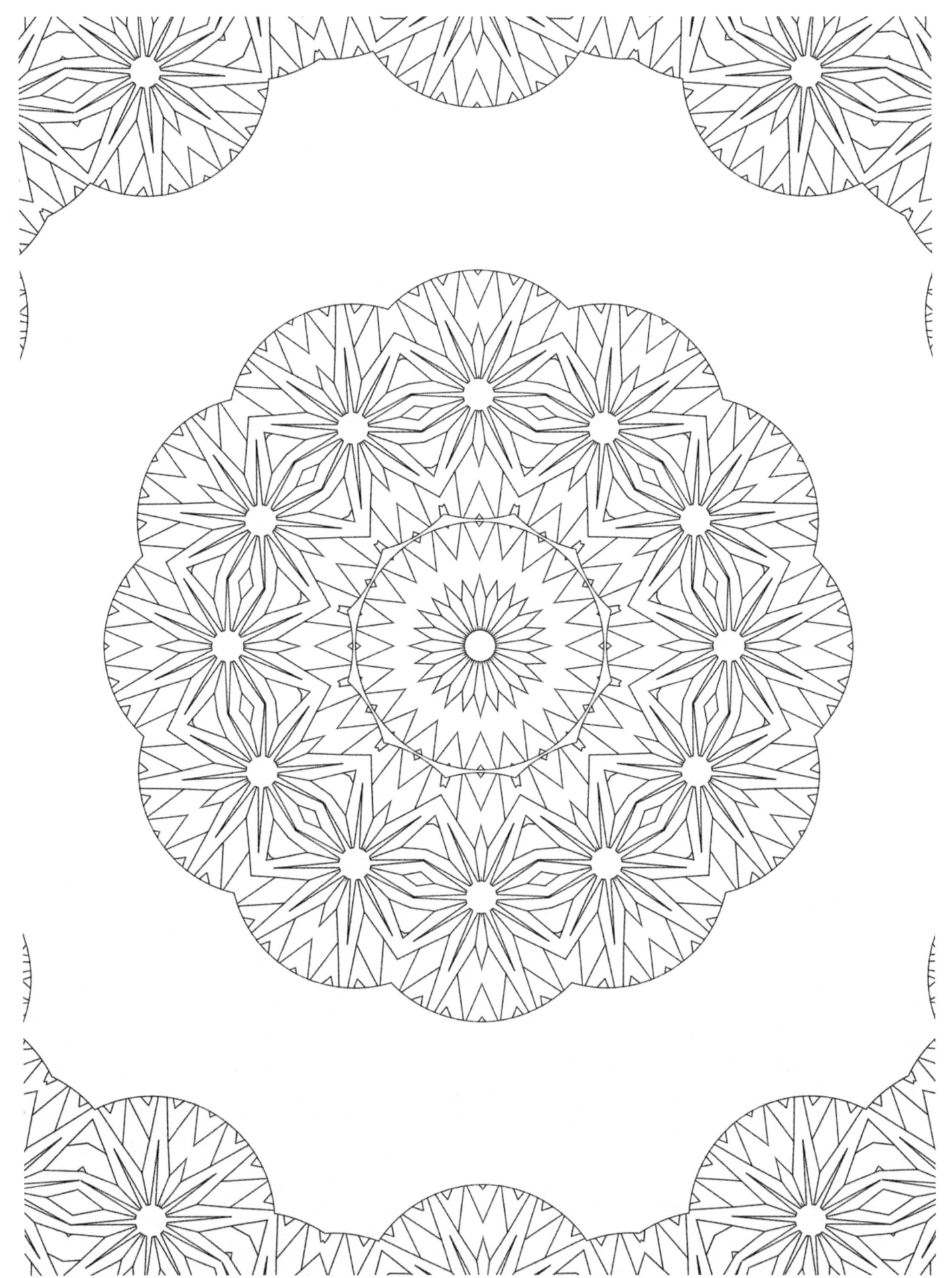

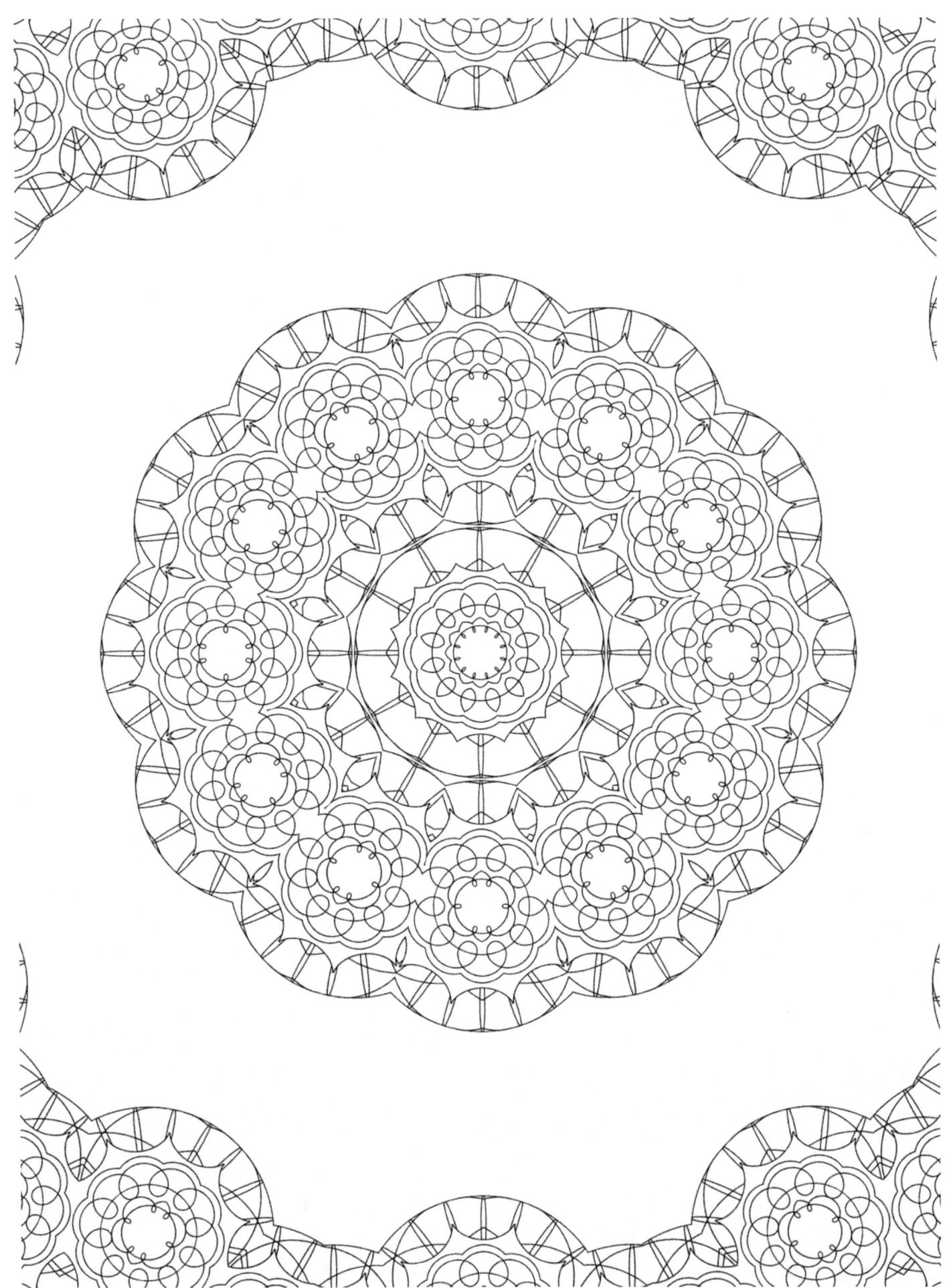

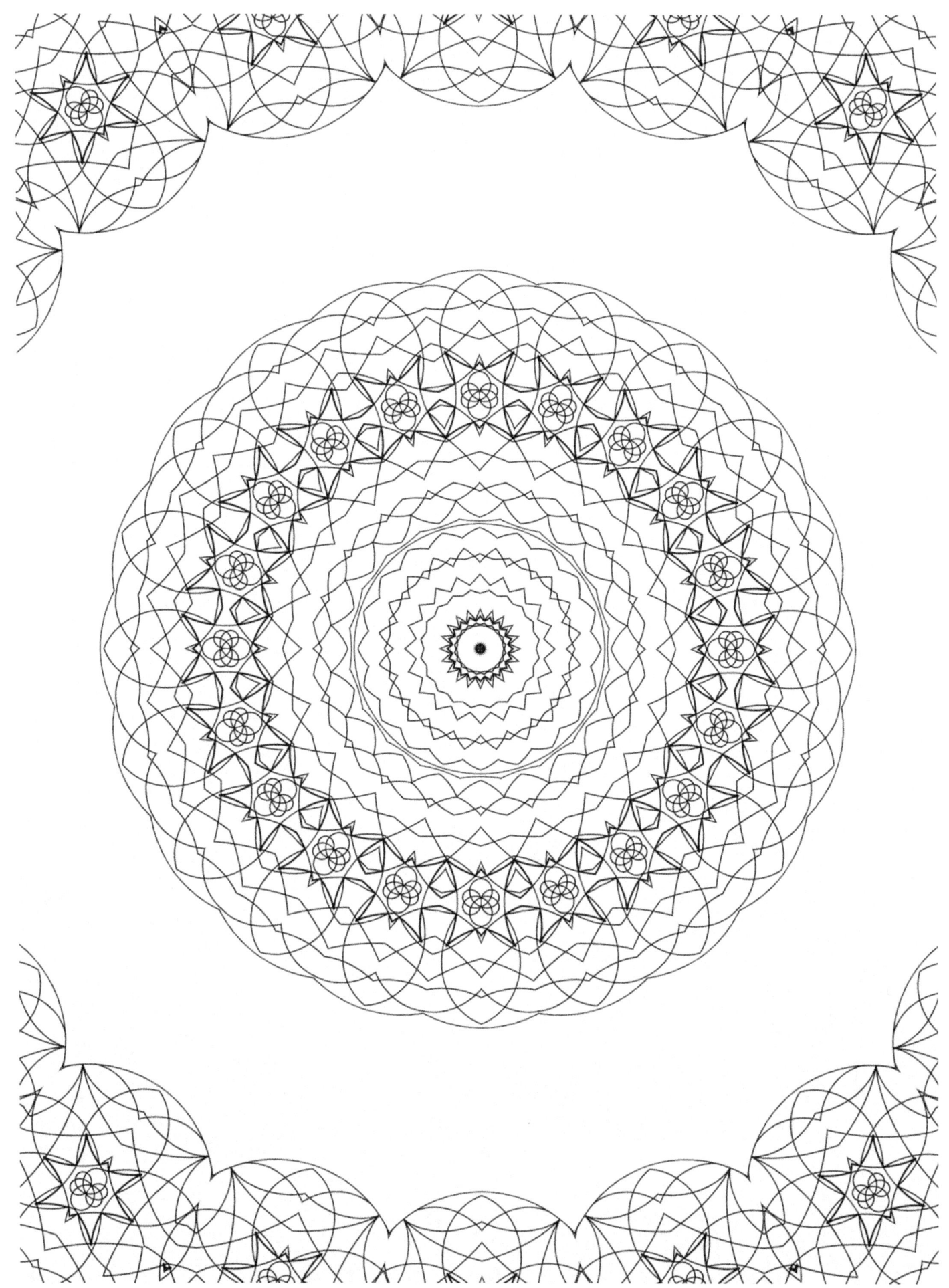

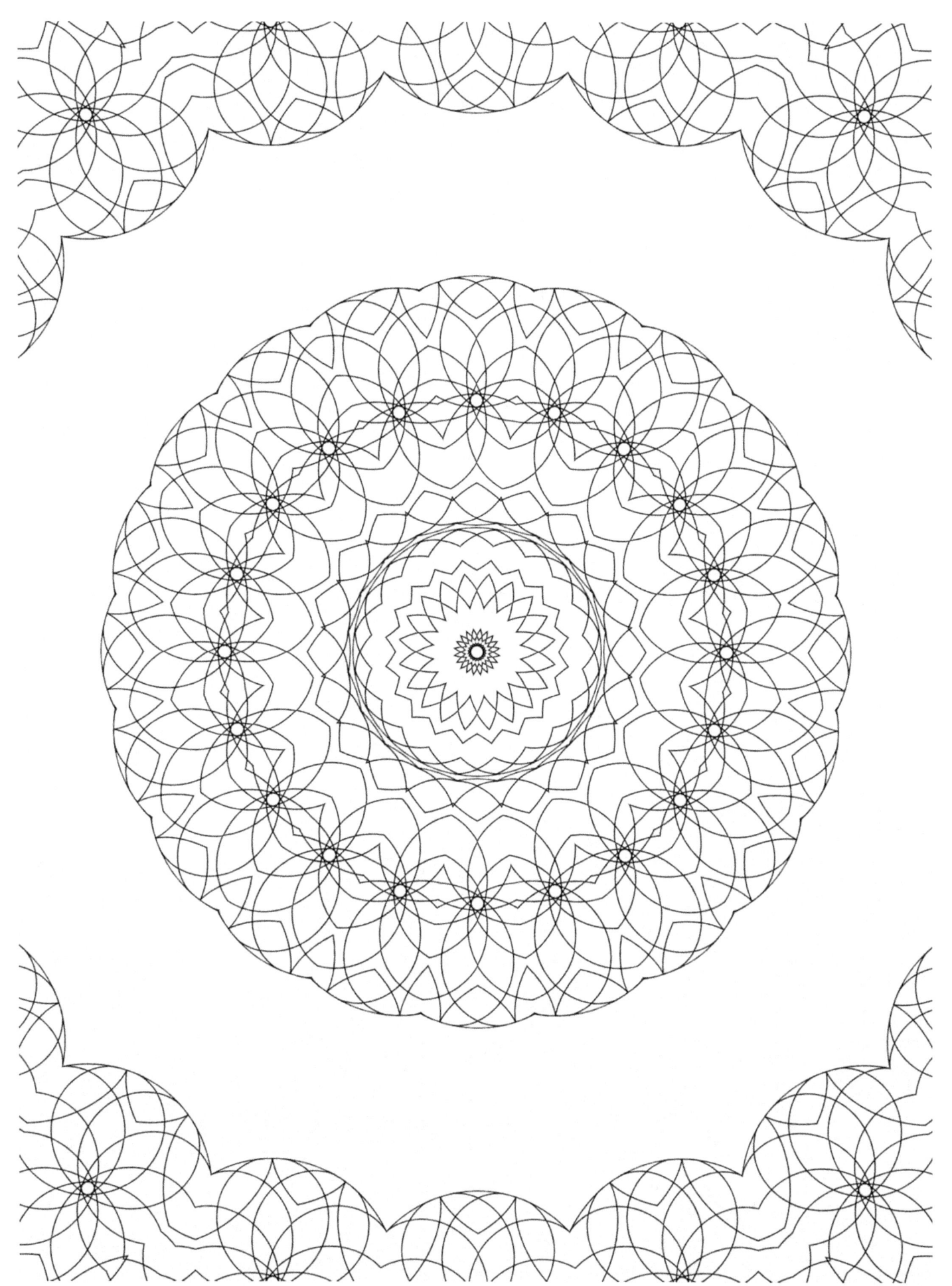

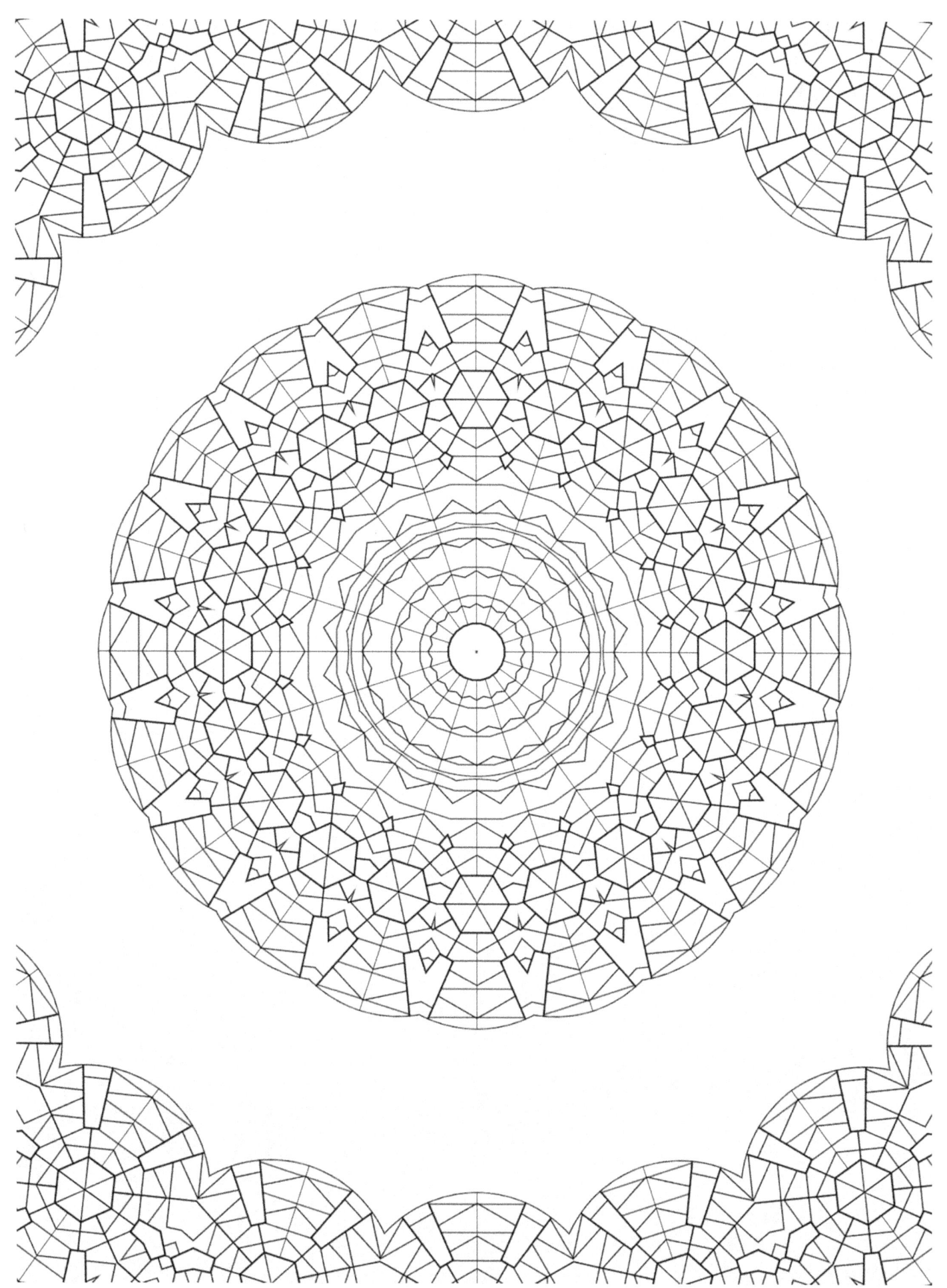

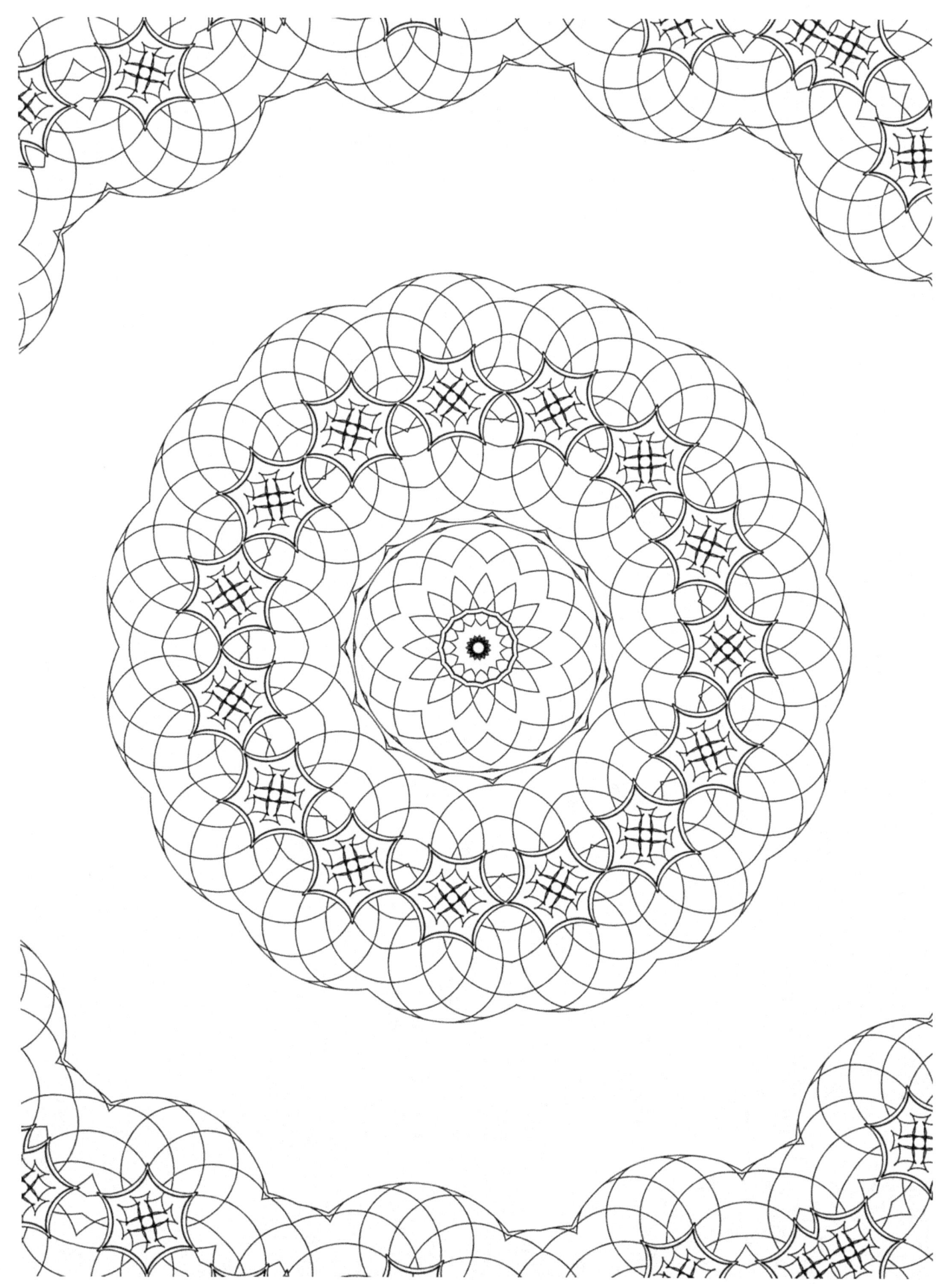

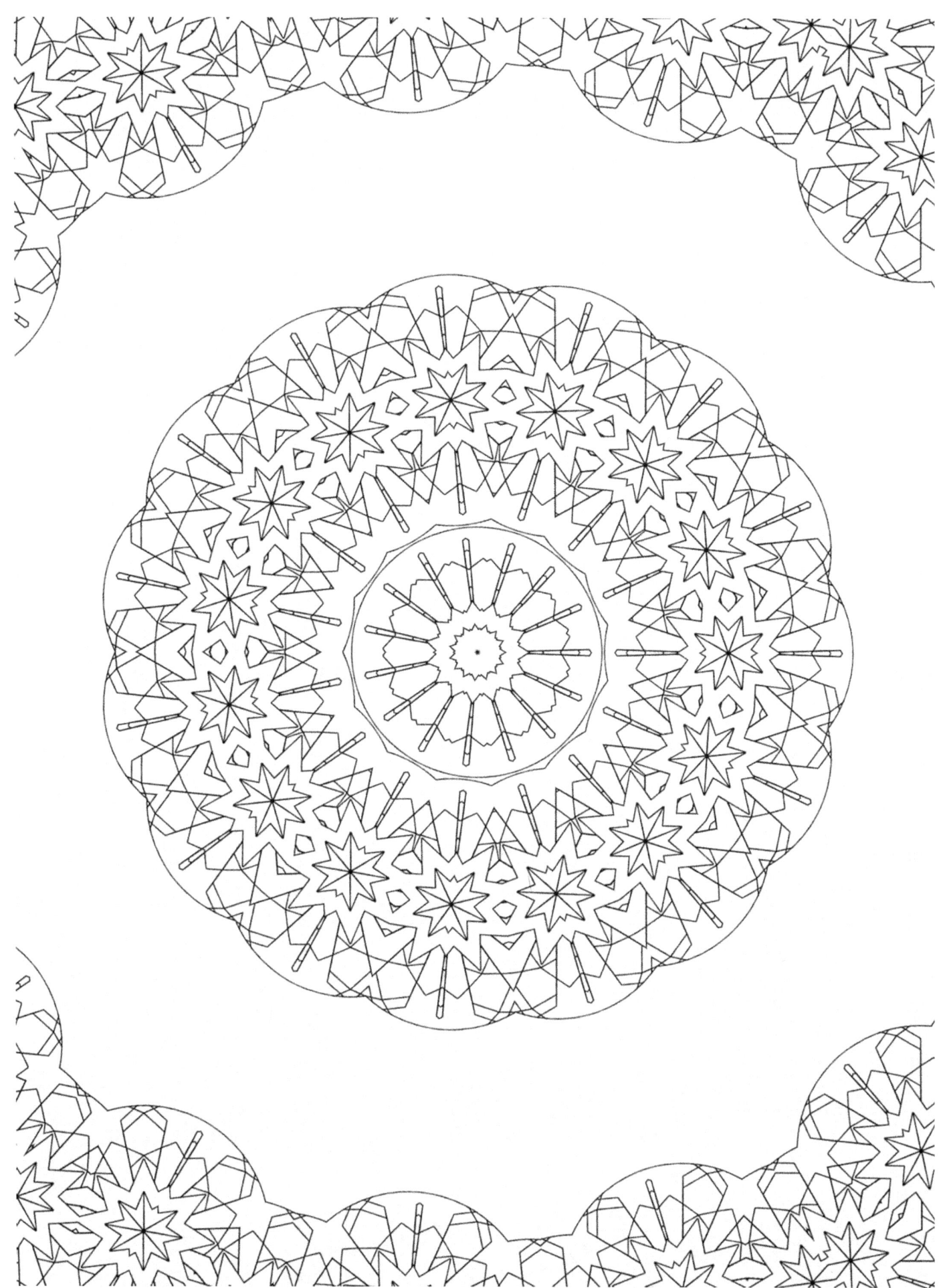

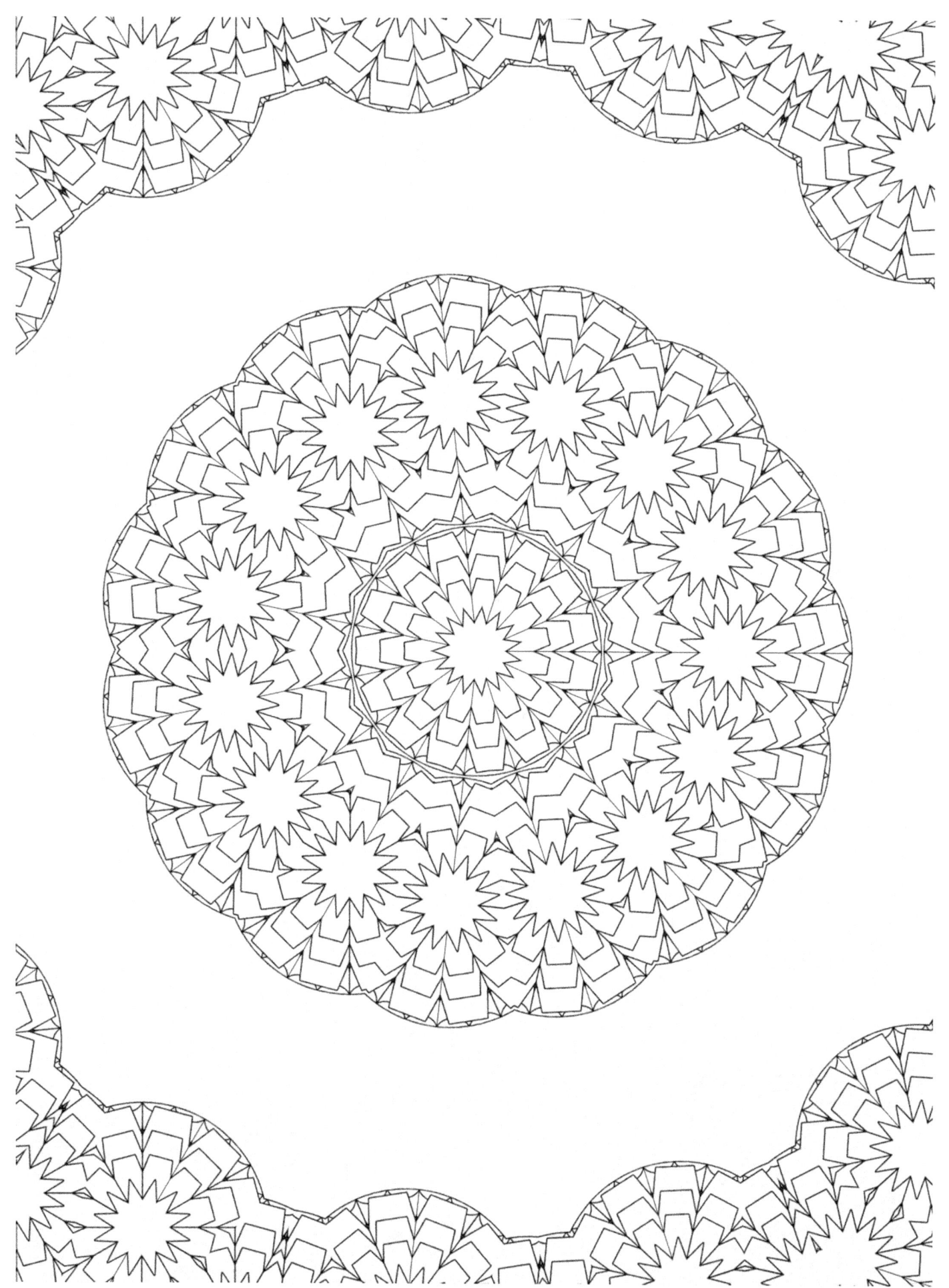

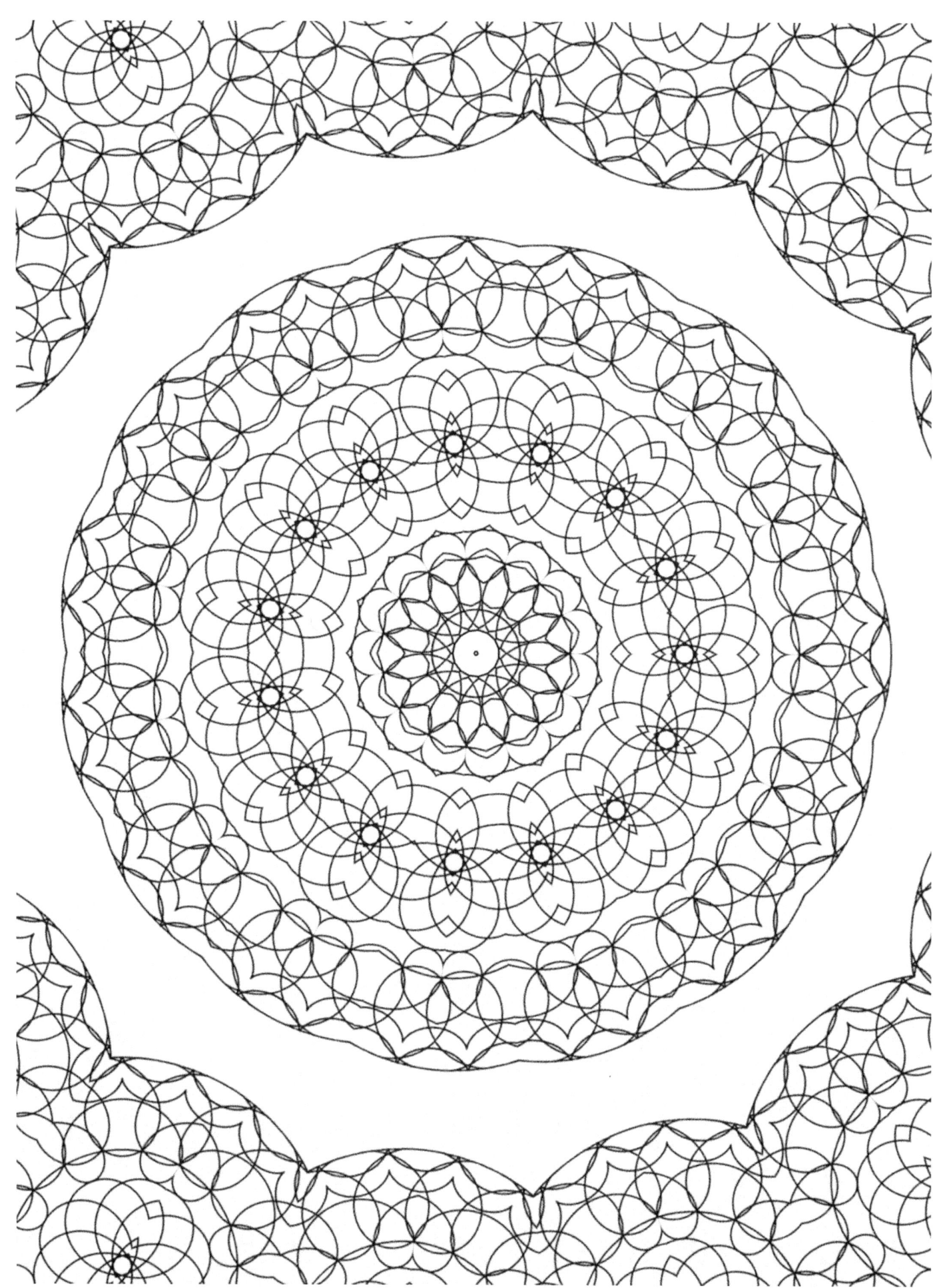

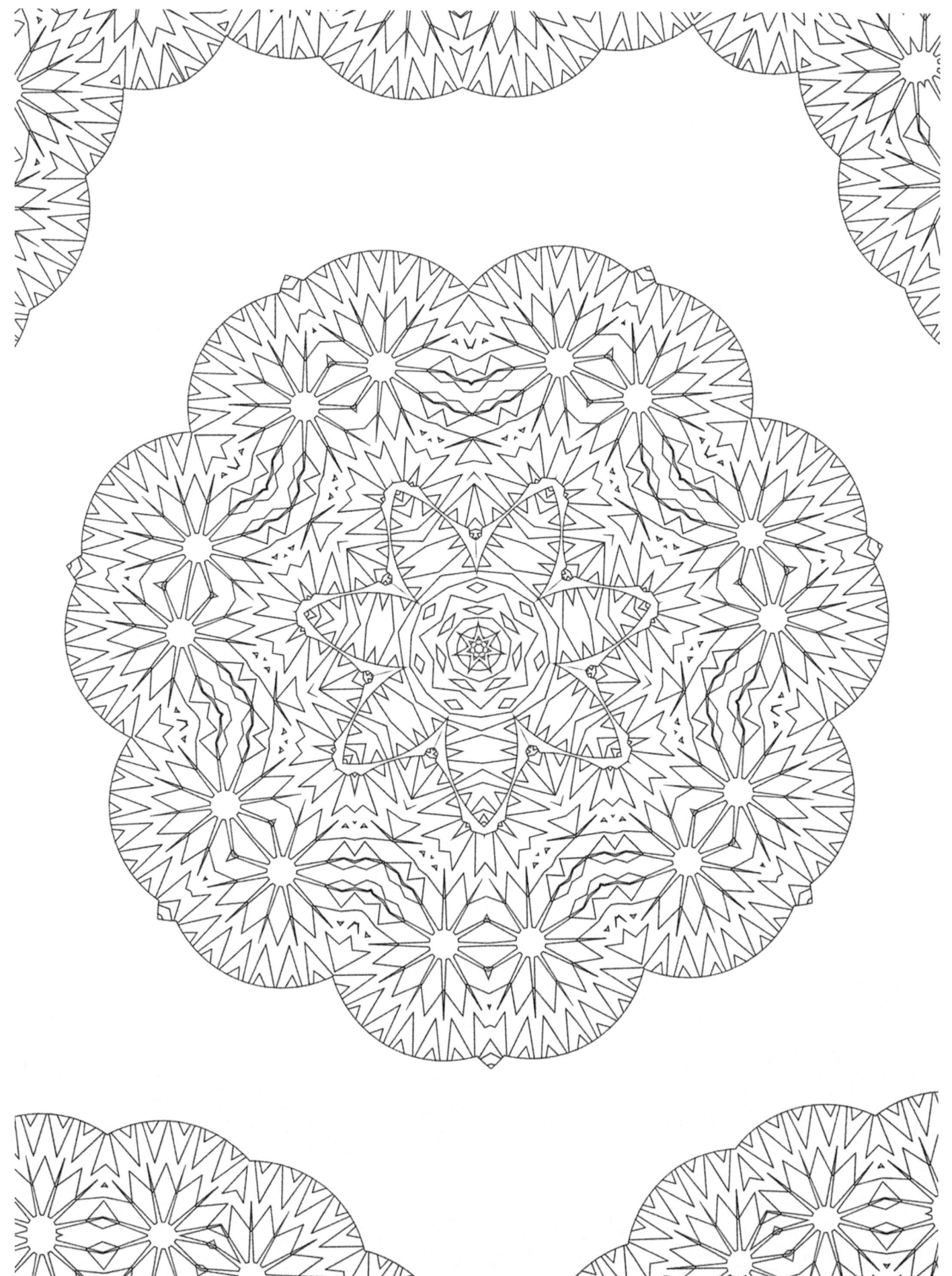

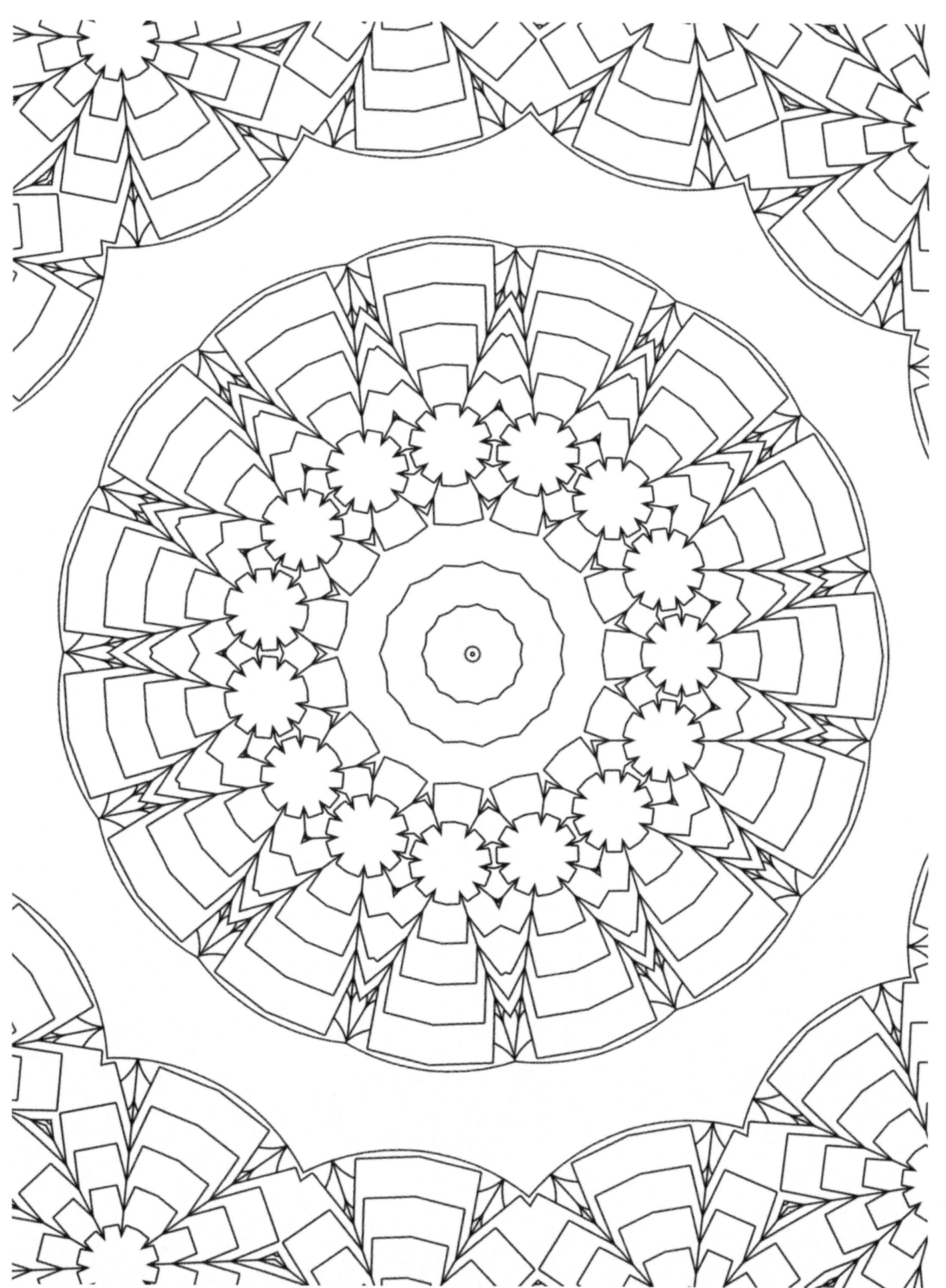

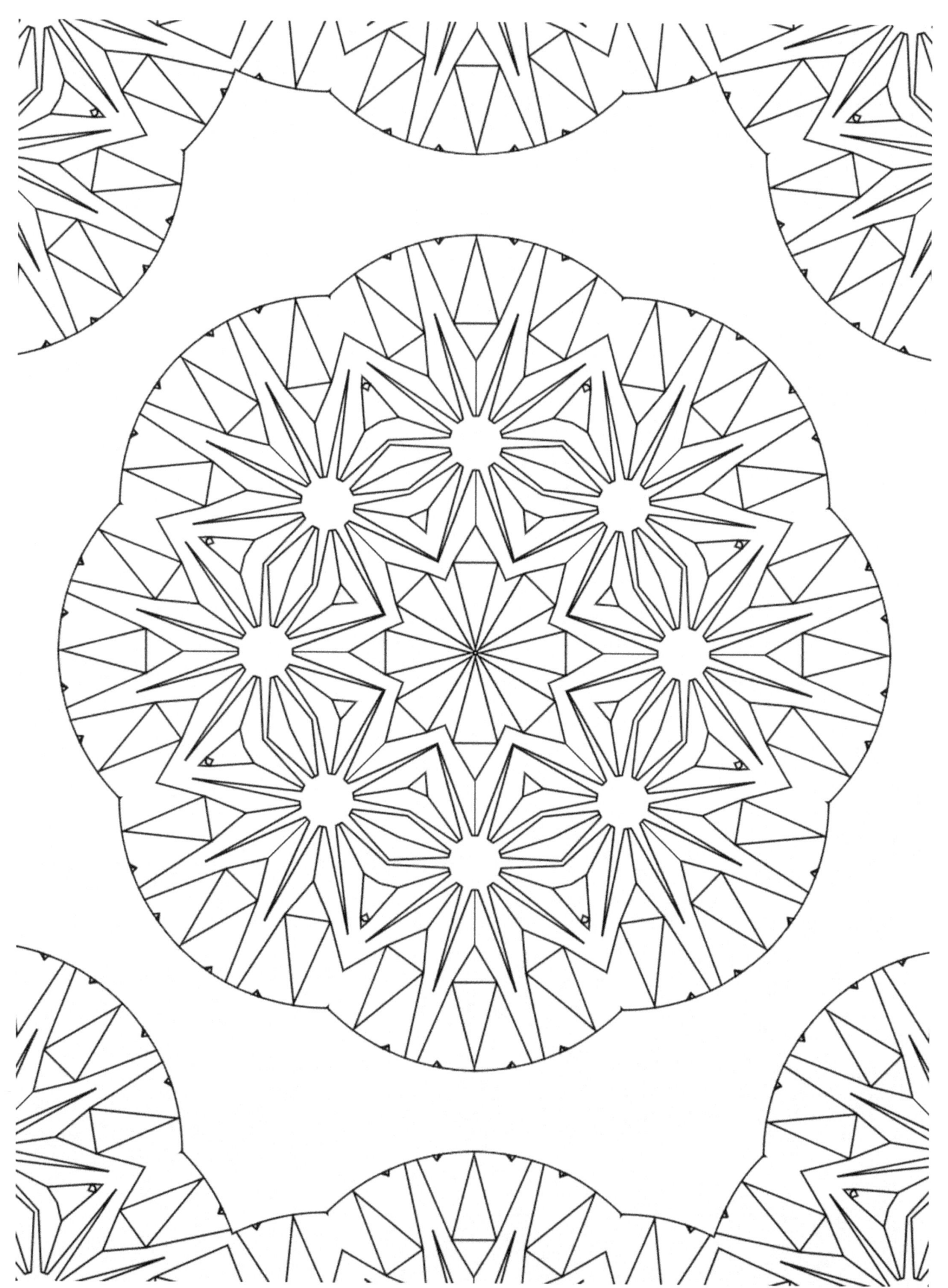

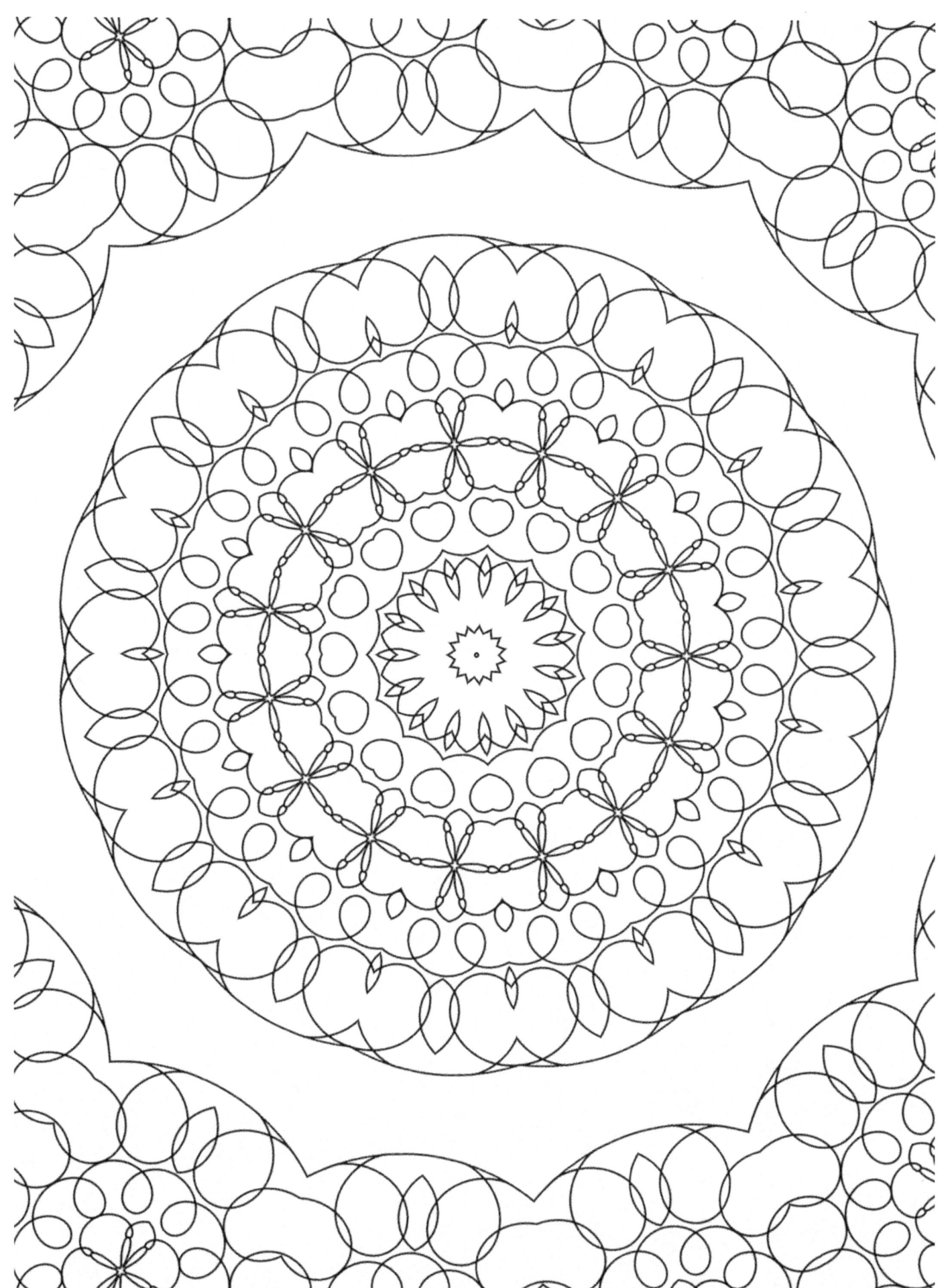

Final Words

If you have enjoyed this puzzle book and are interested in learning more about our other products and publications, please visit:

http://www.colormazen.com/

We design and write -

- Adult Coloring Books
- Mandala Coloring Books
- Pattern Coloring Books
- Sudoku Books
- Puzzle Books
- Crossword Puzzle Books
- Word Search Books
- Planners
- Journals
- Diaries
- Children's Books
- Children's Workbooks